MW00899187

ENDORSEMENTS

"May I invite you to make some time for a conversation with an old friend and dialogue over coffee about what it means to be 'created in the image of God' and how to live in that reality. I plan to put this book by Dr. Lewis on the table by my favorite chair and pause more often with a trusted friend to celebrate the presence of a restoring God."

— *Dr. Ray Woodard, Send City Missionary,*
Vancouver, British Columbia

"I am blessed by the creative ways Dr. Kirk Lewis expresses himself with the printed word. In *God's Mirror Image* he takes the numerous aspects of Jesus' character and presents them in a devotional format. You will be blessed as you read and apply these truths to your life."

— *Larry Bertrand, Associate Pastor,*
Tallowood Baptist Church, Houston

"While reading Dr. Lewis' books, I feel like I'm experiencing the story, feeling the emotions, seeing the amazement in his disciples' eyes as Jesus teaches about our Creator. Lewis has a way of helping us understand Jesus; a way of writing that makes one want to know Jesus; to really try to follow Jesus. Also, he makes me smile. I highly recommend this book."

— *Joann Hutton, Layperson, Harvest United*
Methodist Church, Missouri City, TX.

"Looking for devotional thoughts that will challenge you? Look no further! In his third book, *God's Mirror Image*, Dr. Kirk Lewis brings scripture to life with his self-examining applications and a creative style reminiscent of Max Lucado."

— *Dr. Dan Curry, Pastor, South Oaks Church, Arlington, TX, (Retired) and Area Representative, Baptist General Convention of Texas*

"*God's Mirror Image* is a book you will read repeatedly because it speaks to a question so many Christian's ask. How do we live as a reflection of God's image in today's world? What does that image even look like in us? Lewis offers some of the clearest thinking on the actual process of seeking God's will I've ever read."

— *Nancy Beaulieu, Layperson, Wesley United Methodist Church, Beaumont, TX*

GOD'S MIRROR IMAGE

GOD'S MIRROR IMAGE

15 Ways You Can Live a Christ-Like Life

Dr. Kirk Lewis

XULON PRESS

Xulon Press
2301 Lucien Way #415
Maitland, FL 32751
407.339.4217
www.xulonpress.com

© 2018 by Kirk Lewis

All rights reserved solely by the author. The author guarantees all
contents are original and do not infringe upon the legal rights of any
other person or work. No part of this book may be reproduced in any
form without the permission of the author. The views expressed in this
book are not necessarily those of the publisher.

Unless otherwise indicated, Scripture quotations taken from the Holy
Bible, New International Version (NIV). Copyright © 1973, 1978, 1984,
2011 by Biblica, Inc.™. Used by permission. All rights reserved.

Printed in the United States of America.

ISBN-13: 978-1-54564-908-4

Other Books and Writings

by Dr. Kirk Lewis

Put Away Childish Things

Published 2013 by Xulon Press

The Chase

Our Passionate Pursuit of Life Worth Living

Published 2015 by Xulon Press

The Searcher

A Devotional Blog

www.drkirklewis.com

PREFACE

Our world is an ominous and chaotic place. Politically fractured. Racially charged. Socially divided. Urged into further disarray by a polarized media and intrusive social platforms all-too-often fueled by all-too-prevalent, ill-informed personal biases. We mourn the loss of civility in discourse and debate. Cloaked in righteous fervor, too many Christians feed the monster into which our society is morphing.

It makes me sad that I sometimes get caught up in the moment and contribute to the mayhem. It saddens me more that I, and other Christians, misunderstand what it means to be Christ-like; we see a slow and steady decline in baptisms, church membership, worship attendance and mission giving. In essence, a decline in the Christian faith.

How can we be like Christ and behave the way we too often behave? The answer is simple. We can't. We shouldn't.

I am not a theologian. I'm not a biblical scholar. I'm simply a layman trying to figure things out. The focus of my Bible study over the past year has been the idea of being made in the image of God. I think it has profound implications for how the faith will be perceived in the decades to come.

It's not an easy concept to grasp. God is so. . .out there. As *Monty Python's The Meaning of Life* suggested in one of its farcical prayers, "God, you are so huge."

To be in the image of God seems to be such a deep theological concept. Yet, the promise of Jesus resonates in its simplicity. *"If you have seen me, you have seen the Father."*

Once we get past the wonder of Emmanuel, *"God with us,"* and embrace the character and teachings of Christ, we can see exactly how we exist as God's reflected image in the world. We mirror the image of God by imitating the character of Christ.

I treasure the statement of Mark, who said if all the stories about Jesus and all the things he said were written down, you couldn't build a library big enough to contain them. That bit of gospel hyperbole intrigues me each time I read a passage of scripture. Each story shared about Christ is merely a snippet of that moment in time. A synopsis of what had to be an extended interaction and conversation.

Each chapter of this book speaks to a specific character trait of Jesus that the world needs to see reflected in us each and every day. I may use a bit of imagination to flesh out the stories a little, but I try hard to remain true to the scripture and to what God is teaching me through it. With each new idea, each moment of clarity, comes a new lesson in living. This proves to me that we are never too old to grow in our relationship to God, the Father, through his Son, Jesus Christ.

This book is a slight departure from my first two books, *Put Away Childish Things* and *The Chase*. The blended style is a little different, but I hope the message remains focused on the power we draw from our Father to live like we belong to him each and every day. I pray you find it helpful as you seek to be more like Christ.

ACKNOWLEDGEMENTS

I was never quite sure this book was going to happen. Misplaced trust in a new publishing company tainted my taste for the work. I continued writing my blog with occasional thoughts of quitting that as well.

Whenever I wanted to pull the trigger and just set writing aside, I would get a positive comment from someone who read one of my books or a sweet note from someone who found the Bible studies in *The Searcher* particularly meaningful. Those unexpected blessings, coupled with a little nagging from a friend or two, convinced me to compile a new work.

Thank you to all those who took the time to pass along a note or share a thought about my writing. You were the spark that rekindled the flame.

DEDICATION

To my four young grandchildren,
Eli, Josiah, Lena and Amelia.
With all the love in my heart for each of you,
I look forward to the day when you put your
faith and trust in Jesus as your personal savior.
No longer just grandchildren,
but brothers and sisters in Christ.

TABLE OF CONTENTS

A Roadmap to a Christ-Like Life 1

A Life of Self-Sacrifice...9

A Life that Always Does Good...16

A Life of Complete Devotion...28

A Life of Discipline in the Face of Temptation.........................36

A Life of Service Above Self..43

A Life of Spiritual Influence..50

A Life of Forgiveness 60

A Life Spent Thirsting for Righteousness.................................69

A Life of Integrity 79

A Life of Peace, Love & Joy..88

A Life of Compassion 96

A Life of Deeply Rooted Faith..103

A Life of Empathy 119

Like Father, Like Son 124

A ROADMAP TO
A CHRIST-LIKE LIFE

Background Passages:
Genesis 1:27; John 14:9; Matthew 5:1-12

I pored through a number of old 35mm slides, pictures taken by my parents when my siblings and I were small. I enjoyed sharing those captured memories with my children and grandchildren. Fascination grew as we recognized family resemblances across generations. . .the power of genetics, I suppose. If I heard it once, I heard it several times: "I see your Dad in his eyes." "You look so much like your uncle at that age." "She is the spitting image of your mother."

There is some measure of joy in knowing that we physically resemble those most dear to us. Then, I wonder, when others look at us, do they see how closely we resemble Christ in spirit and deed? Can the world see Jesus. . .see God. . .in us?

> *"So God created man in his own image,*
>
> *in the image of God he created him;*
>
> *male and female he created them."*

On the surface, being created in the image of God seems to be such a complex theological concept requiring a deeper understanding of the nature and spirit of the Creator himself. But it's really not that hard. Jesus told his disciples, *"If you have seen me, you have seen the Father."* In other words, we find in the character of Jesus Christ the very nature and spirit of God. The image of God reflected in the life of Christ. Being the image of God in our world, as we were created to be, simply requires us to be like Jesus.

So how are we to know what that looks like?

Every gospel story reveals the character of Christ. We can identify in Jesus God's compassion, love, faith, humility and honesty. We find in his teachings keys to living as the image of God.

People flocked to Jesus early in his ministry in Galilee, drawn by the candor and consistency of his teaching and the power of his healing. As he left Capernaum one day, the crowd pressed around him to hear his words and feel his touch. Eventually, somewhere on the northeastern shore of the Sea of Galilee, he sat down on a rocky hillside and began to teach. Matthew records this event as the Sermon on the Mount.

Rather than a single event, the Sermon on the Mount may be a collection of ideas that Jesus taught over and over throughout his ministry that Matthew captured as a summary of his teaching themes. William Barclay, in his commentaries, suggests as much.

One of the most beloved segments of these verses is known as The Beatitudes, a passage that unveils the character demanded of those who desire to be a part of the kingdom of God. When you look at the passage and look at the life of Christ, you'll find that Jesus modeled each character trait in his daily walk.

Blessed are the poor in spirit, for theirs is the kingdom of God.
Blessed are those who mourn, for they will be comforted.
Blessed are the meek, for they will inherit the earth.
Blessed are those who hunger and thirst after righteousness,
for they will be filled.
Blessed are the merciful, for they shall be shown mercy.
Blessed are the pure in heart, for they will see God.
Blessed are the peacemakers, for they will be called the sons of God.
Blessed are those who are persecuted because of righteousness,
for theirs is the kingdom of heaven.

Jesus teaches about living in the kingdom of God. Think of these statements as proverbs or declarations. Assuring us that we will feel blessed as a result of our actions or attitudes that align with the expectations of the Father. That demonstrating these character traits leads to promised rewards.

Consider the word "blessed." Some translations substitute the word "happy" for "blessed." But "happy" feels too frivolous. Too superficial. Think, rather, of the contentment, joy and peace that come from being in a right relationship with God. These cannot be dampened by external circumstances. Happiness may be a part of the equation, but take it deeper into the heart of our relationship with the Father. One commentary called being blessed "a pledge of divine reward for the inner spiritual character of the righteous." I like that. Jesus promises that if we live in such a way as to reflect the character of Christ, we will be filled with inner peace and joy.

Focus on the specific character demanded of those who would be part of the kingdom of God and the promise that follows. Blessed are. . .

. . .the poor in spirit.

To be poor in a financial sense is to be destitute. To be poor in a physical sense is to be oppressed. To be poor in spirit is to be humbled, to live without arrogance or self-sufficiency. This speaks to the person who recognizes his or her sinful nature; who comes to God each day with a contrite heart; knowing that God's grace is an unmerited gift that promises a life within the kingdom of God.

. . .those who mourn.

Everyone in this life will experience sadness and grief. Such mourning is a natural part of the ebb and flow of life. Here, Jesus speaks of those who mourn for a lost world; for the sinfulness that serves as a barrier separating us from God. . .from the relationship he desired with us when he created us. If we don't grieve for the lost, we will never feel compelled to share the love of Christ with a ruined world. God will provide comfort for those whose hearts break when confronted by sin and disbelief. Comfort that allows us to continue the hard work of reconciling a lost world with the one who loves it so much.

4

. . .the meek.

Think of meekness not as passivity or weakness. That is the world's definition. Its first-century meaning carries an idea of self-control. . .gentleness. . .kindness. . .all fruits of the spirit identified by Paul. The meek control their instincts and impulses, harnessing the passion and power within them to build and edify, to lift up rather than tear down. They see all things through the eyes of empathy, hearts free of evil intent and purpose. These are people who treat everyone with respect and dignity regardless of their station in life.

. . .those who hunger and thirst after righteousness.

Hunger and thirst represent our most primal needs. When truly hungry and thirsty, a body will do almost anything to secure food or drink. Little else seems to matter. To hunger and thirst for righteousness is to demonstrate that strongest spiritual desire to understand and act upon the will of God. Our passion to live for him takes precedence over anything else. Therein lies the promise. The one who seeks after God will have those needs satisfied. His or her life will be filled with the joy of knowing who walks beside us.

. . .the merciful.

Mercy is an act of grace. Despite our sinful ways, God offers his forgiveness, requiring only a contrite heart. It is pure, unmerited grace. Mercy is not a quality limited to God. As believers in Christ discover his forgiveness, mercy toward others ought to be a natural outgrowth of our hearts. People hurt us. Ignore us. Sin against us. Hate us. Persecute us. We face a choice: retaliate or redeem. Mercy finds expression in the kindness and compassion we extend even to those who hurt us. It is a quality borne of the mercy God extends to us even when we hurt him. As we forgive, so are we forgiven. That is the promise of God.

. . .the pure in heart.

When the Bible speaks of the heart, it speaks of the center of will, the choices we make. Pure in heart means that the decisions we make, the desires we hold, the intent of our thoughts and deeds must be unblemished by sin, wholly pleasing to God. The purity of our hearts lies at the center of every characteristic proclaimed in The Beatitudes. . .our mercy, our quest for righteousness, our meekness and humility. Jesus told Nicodemus, "You must be born again" to suggest a spiritual change in his heart. To take that which was unclean and purify it from all self-interests and desires.

Jesus promises those who will listen that the pure in heart will see God. There is certainly within this statement a promise of our eternal life in the presence of the Father. It might also suggest that the pure in heart have within them the capacity to see God in every circumstance. . .seeing his presence in life's heartbreaks and horrors as well as its blessings and bounty.

. . .the peacemakers.

The kingdom of God is a kingdom of peace, yet we are too often at war with one another. The broken relationships, the societal divisions, the political acrimony, the racial bigotry drive a wedge between God's people. Joy comes to those who find ways of bringing people together in the love of Christ, reconciling others with God and one another. This statement promises that the peacemakers will be called "Sons of God." The Old Testament called angels the "Sons of God." Angels may be an apt description of those who act as God's peacemakers.

. . .the persecuted.

Living a lifestyle exemplified by the characteristics listed in The Beatitudes puts one in a precarious place. The life God demands of his children is a life the world opposes and rejects. All who identify with Christ face a hostile world that tolerates them in the best of times and terrorizes them in the worst of times. God offers a promise to those who face such opposition. Hold on. Run the race. Keep the faith. God's kingdom is yours forever.

I go back to the beginning. We are to live as the image of God. That's how he created us. We discover how to do that by looking at the life of Christ and paying attention to his teachings. Throughout his ministry, Jesus taught us how to live and modeled those choices every day of his life. He lived and breathed every action and attitude he taught in The Beatitudes. If we are to live like him, as the image of God, we ought to do the same.

The promise of The Beatitudes is not a pie-in-the-sky, wait-for-it kind of promise. Barclay writes: ". . .the Beatitudes are not pious hopes of what shall be; they are not glowing but nebulous prophecies of some future bliss; they are congratulations on what is. . . .It is a blessedness (a joy and peace) which exists here and now."

Live it!

Claim the promise!

A LIFE OF SELF-SACRIFICE

Background Passages:
Mark 8:27-36; Luke 9:18-25

The Master slipped to the grass,
sliding from the flat rock upon which he had sat
as he spent the last hour in prayer.
The canopy of trees under which he now reclined,
his back against the rock,
sheltered him from the late afternoon sun.

Jesus glanced at his disciples.
Gathered in a loose cluster 40 feet down the hill.
As they finished their prayers one by one,
they talked quietly among themselves,
breaking a small loaf of bread.
Passing it around.
Satisfying their hunger.

Jesus looked past his disciples
into the town of Caesarea Philippi,
a bustling city 30 miles north of the region of Galilee.
Watched the frenetic pace of the people as they

finished the work of the day and
headed home.

He lifted his eyes toward the sheer cliff
north of the city, rising 150 feet above the
lush, green valley below.
The stream gushing from the massive grotto
on the western edge of the cliff
served as the headwaters of the Jordan River
as it flowed south to the Sea of Galilee.

From his vantage point above the cliff,
Jesus could see into the cavern,
rumored to be the birthplace of Pan,
the Greek god of nature.
Worshippers still brought offerings of fruit and grain,
laying them at the altar.
His vision shifted to the pagan temple.
Gleaming, white marble, reflecting the sun.
Philip, the region's ruler, had dedicated it to
Caesar Augustus,
the Roman emperor considered a god by Roman citizens.
Even before the Romans built the altars,
Jesus knew whole area stood as a religious center
dedicated to the worship of Baal,
the ancient Canaanite god.

Deeply reflective.
Jesus contemplated the scene spread across the valley below.
Considered all he had done during his ministry.
Felt his gut tighten when he thought

about the cross to come.
Had anything he said and done made a difference?
Before he began his final journey to the cross,
Jesus needed to know.
Did anyone really know who he was?

The disciples talked quietly,
laughing in the ease of friendships
forged by common experiences.
Jesus cut through the
comfortable conversation.
"Who do the crowds say I am?"

*****

It was a leading question, designed to get to the heart of their hearts. Surrounded by the trappings of pagan worship, Jesus called his disciples think deeply about what they had seen and heard. To reflect seriously on what they believed.

You can almost hear the rustle of robes and the shuffle of feet as they turned toward Jesus. They were used to his probing. Knew an answer was required. "John the Baptist," one blurted. "One of the old prophets brought back to life," announced another. "Elijah," another proudly proclaimed.

Jesus glanced again at the city below, lost in thought for a moment. Then he turned back to his disciples. "But what about you? Who do you say I am?" It was the perfect question for a perfect point in time.

Jesus held his breath, looking into the eyes of each of his closest friends. Their answers would make all the difference. Would he see blank stares of incomprehension? Would he catch so much as a spark of understanding that meant he had at least lit a torch in their hearts? He waited. Felt his heart thump anxiously in his chest.

How his soul must have soared when Peter stood among them, looked at his friends, then to Jesus, knowing that he answered for all of them. "You are the Messiah. The Anointed One of God."

That moment sealed the deal for Jesus. He then taught them intently about the events to come.

Suffering.
Rejection.
Death.
Resurrection.

Prophecies that left them frightened and confused. Then he challenged them with words that echo still in the ears of every believer today.

"If anyone would come after me, he must deny himself and take up his cross daily and follow me. For whoever wants to save his life will lose it, but whoever loses his life for me will save it. What does it profit a man to gain the whole world and yet lose or forfeit his very soul?"

Denial of self. No one did that more completely than Jesus Christ. If living in the image of God is to live as Christ, then the call of Christ demands that we deny ourselves. It's not a matter of dismissing our lives as unworthy or inconsequential in the grand scheme of God's plan. Denying ourselves means setting aside our egos. Deliberately subordinating our wills to the will of God. Opening our lives to the possibility that his plan for us is greater and more meaningful than the one we planned for ourselves. It means turning from where we wish to go to follow the path he lays before us.

The call of Christ demands that we take up his cross. Not just *any* cross. . .*his* cross. Jesus knew the horror of what lay before him. When Jesus was a boy, a Jewish rebellion in Sepphoris, just four miles from Nazareth, ended badly for those who fought against the Roman Empire. Historians tell us that more than 2,000 rebels were crucified, set in lines along the roadside as a frightful reminder of the power of Rome.

To face the cross was a vicious reality burned into the back of his mind. He as well as anyone knew what it meant to take up the cross. It stood as the inevitable certainty he faced by declaring a kingdom of God that rocked the boats of the pious and the political.

Today, taking up the cross of Christ means living our lives with the same focused commitment to God's purpose that Jesus did. It means preparing for rejection in a world that does not understand. Letting nothing. . .no thought of ridicule, persecution or embarrassment. . .prevent us from doing that which we know God desires us to do. It means looking at a world that dismisses Jesus as irrelevant and proclaiming in word and deed, "I belong to Christ!"

Denying ourselves.

Taking up his cross.

These are steps in the right direction. If we stop there, however, we miss that which matters most. The call of Christ demands we follow. It means spending our lives, not hoarding them. It means giving of ourselves, not taking from others. It means not playing it safe, but doing the right thing at all times and in all situations. It means not getting by with as little as we can for the cause of Christ, but investing ourselves completely in his ministry.

The way of the world is always to seek to gain advantage over another. The goal of the world is to amass more wealth, power and glory than the guy next door. Jesus would answer that unbridled ambition with this question: Where is the eternal profit in that way of life? Jesus said a man saves his life when he loses it in service to others.

As believers in Christ, we have been called to follow the lead of Christ, not always knowing where it will take us. Doors open and doors close. Following his lead is not always easy, but it is always best.

I'm reminded of the old invitational hymn *Wherever He Leads, I'll Go,* written in 1936 by Baylus Benjamin McKinney. He penned the words of his poem after meeting with the Rev. R.S. Jones, a South American missionary who had been pulled from service because of a serious illness and would not be allowed to return.

"What will you do?" McKinney asked his friend.

"I don't know, but wherever he leads, I'll go."

From a simple conversation between two old friends poured the words that challenge us. . .challenge me. . .today. It is "my heart, my life, my all" I must bring to "Christ who loves me so." I must declare him "master, Lord and king" before I can promise "wherever he leads I'll go."

The chorus of the song implores me to "follow my Christ" simply because "he loves me so." I can think of no better reason.

So, wherever he leads, let's go.

A LIFE THAT ALWAYS DOES GOOD

Background Passages:
Matthew 12:1-14; Mark 2:23-3:6; Luke 6:1-12

I read another news account this week about the Baptist church in Kansas staging another protest to condemn with unholy words those they deem to be sinners responsible for the ruin of the world. Citing scripture. Calling names. Their views right. All others wrong. Compassion lost to the certainty of their conviction.

I don't understand it. How can a people claiming to be of God miss so badly the spirit of God? How can they interpret scripture so strictly that they fail to see the hurt they inflict?

Their actions this week reminded me of a story from scripture. Journey with me to Capernaum.

*****

He watched from the shadows of the alley
between two homes.

The healer wound his way through the streets of
Capernaum,
a gathering crowd surrounding him
and his closest friends.

The man darted from house to house,
staying just ahead of Jesus.
Always in shadows cast by the rising sun.
Unnoticed.
That's the way he liked it.
When people noticed,
they stared.
When people noticed,
they judged.

No warning!
Someone grabbed his left arm,
startling the man.
Dark brown eyes under bushy eyebrows
stared into his own.
The elegant robe told him all he needed to know.
A Pharisee.
He recognized him as one of the priests from Jerusalem
following in the footsteps of the healer
for the past three weeks.

"Come with me,"
commanded the priest,
pulling him down the alley
into deeper darkness.

The priest looked at the man's withered right hand.

It dangled uselessly at the end of an arm.
Lacking any strength.
Nodding at his infirmity, the priest asked,
"How did that happen?"

"I was kicked by a donkey eight years ago.
I can no longer use my hand."

"I have a proposition for you. . ."
started the Pharisee,
explaining his plan.
A furtive glance.
A smile that lacked sincerity.
The priest slinked away.
The man with the shriveled hand
did as he was instructed.
Went to the synagogue to wait for the healer.
Stood by the entrance to the white-stoned building,
waiting for Jesus.

As Jesus approached,
the man stepped out to greet him.
"Rabbi, I am in need of your healing."
Words the Pharisee told him to speak.

Jesus smiled.
Saw his hand.
The need obvious,
sensing more to the story.
"Why come to me?"

"I've seen what you can do," said the man.

Then, with a nervous glance at the Pharisees
finding a seat in the crowded synagogue,
"They told me you could heal me today."

Jesus looked at the men who
had questioned his every move for weeks.
"Did they now?"

The man.
Oblivious to the obvious,
"I need to provide for my family.
I need to work.
I want to work.
If there is a chance. . . ."
His voice trailed off in an all-too-familiar
whisper of hopelessness.

Jesus looked into his eyes.
Heart full of compassion.
He threw his arm around him,
glancing once more at the Pharisees.
"Come on in.
Find a seat.
Let's see what God will do today."

Jesus walked to the front of the room.
Sat down on the stone bench.
Surveyed the packed room filled with
the contrite.
The curious.
The condemning.
The stage set for another lesson about the

priorities of God.

*****

Read the account of the man with the withered hand in three of the four gospels. The confrontation between the religious leaders and Jesus in the Capernaum synagogue started in the fields that morning on the way to worship. In the end, the Savior's compassion was both rejected and received. It started as an ordinary Sabbath morning.

Jesus and his disciples rose that morning, intent upon going to the synagogue for the Sabbath time of teaching and worship. The local rabbi requested that Jesus lead the discussion, a frequent occurrence early in his ministry.

For days, the Pharisees sent from Jerusalem tagged along everywhere Jesus went, hovering always on the edge of the crowd. Dipping in and out of the conversation when it suited them.

Questioning his motives.

Probing for answers.

Checking Jesus' words against their own rigid interpretation of scripture. Determined to find reasons to discredit his teaching. Hoping to turn the crowds against him.

As the disciples moved along the country path into the village, they walked along the edge of a wheat field. Through stalks of grain ripe for harvest. In the cool of the morning, they absentmindedly plucked heads of grain from the stalks. Rubbed their hands together to remove the husk from the kernels. Blew into their palms to separate the wheat from the chaff. Popped the morsels into their mouths. Hungry men on the way to church.

On any other day, the actions of the disciples would raise no eyebrows. Eating another man's grain along the path was a standard of care for the hungry and weary traveler. But today was the Sabbath. The Pharisees almost giggled in delight. They had caught Jesus' followers violating the strict rules of the Sabbath regarding work. . .harvesting, winnowing and preparing food.

They practically ran over the disciples in their haste to confront Jesus for this egregious violation. This blatant disregard of Sabbath law.

Jesus took the opportunity to teach, hoping his words would resonate. *"Have you not read. . ."* reminding them that David entered the Temple while under duress and took the consecrated bread in order to feed himself and his hungry men.

He quoted Hosea: *"If you had known what these words mean, 'I desire mercy, not sacrifice,' you would not have condemned the innocent."* As the debate ensued, Jesus silenced them. They stood with their mouths opening and closing like fish out of water. No rebuttal.

"The Sabbath is made for man, not man for the Sabbath. For the Son of Man is Lord of the Sabbath."

The day cannot take precedent over human need. The law cannot substitute for mercy. This whole episode troubled Jesus. The conversation lingered in the Savior's heart as he began to teach the lesson that day. A lesson about the priorities of God.

The same Pharisees who hassled Jesus during their walk into town laid a trap for him, taking advantage of a man's disability. Dangling him in front of Jesus. A worm on a hook. Begging Jesus to bite. To heal the man so they could challenge Jesus in a public setting about his contempt for the Sabbath.

Can't you see the Pharisees fidgeting in their seats, waiting for Jesus to take their bait? When he didn't immediately do so, one of them could no longer contain himself. Interrupting Jesus as he taught, he reminded Jesus of the episode in the grain field. He demanded to know: "If, as you say, it's permissible to harvest on the Sabbath. . .

Is it lawful to heal on the Sabbath?"

From the moment he met the man with the withered hand outside the synagogue and heard his story, Jesus expected the question. *"If any of you has a sheep and it falls into a pit on the Sabbath, will you not take hold of it and lift it out? How much more valuable is a person than a sheep!"* The implication clear.

"It is lawful to do good on the Sabbath."

Jesus waited for their response. Jesus had expected the question. They had not expected that answer. So they sat, tight-lipped and tense.

It's hard for 100 people to fall silent, but if a pin had dropped in the sanctuary at that moment, everyone would have heard it. All sat perfectly still. Only their eyes darted back and forth between Jesus and the Pharisees, waiting for the next sandal to fall.

Jesus rose to his feet. Walked to the middle of the room. He looked for the man he had met earlier by the door. He found him, sitting in the corner. Hiding behind the town's burly blacksmith. The Savior caught his eye. Motioned for him to come forward. A smile, warm with compassion. An invitation. Jesus stood behind him. Rested his hands on the man's shoulders. "Stand here with me in front of everyone." In front of these self-righteous men.

With fire in his eyes stoked by their hard-heartedness, Jesus bore into the souls of the Pharisees. Hear a heavy sigh in Jesus' voice as he posed one last question, hoping to elicit a glimmer of understanding from their closed and locked hearts.

"Let me ask you, which is lawful on the Sabbath: to do good or to do evil, to save a life or destroy it?"

Every eye in the room drawn to the obvious. The misshapen and shriveled hand hanging uselessly at the man's side.

In their silence, more contempt. More condemnation.

Jesus looked toward heaven. Eyes closed. Let out a slow breath to purge his gut of the bile of disgust rising in his throat. He spoke softly to the man, little more than a whisper in his ear. *"Stretch out your hand."*

The instant the man followed Jesus' command, the muscles and tendons regained their strength. The gnarled, misshapen fingers relaxed. He raised his hand in front of his face, flexed his fingers. Completely restored. Strong and sound like the other. Healthy again. Productive again. The synagogue erupted in shouts of joy from the people gathered to worship.

In a huff, unable to celebrate a life made whole, the Pharisees stormed out to conspire with bitter enemies to plot the death of Jesus.

*****

When we read these stories, we tend to look at them only as episodes chronicling the growing confrontation between Jesus and the religious leaders. If that were all it was, I'm not sure all three gospels would have carried an account of the story. There is a deeper, richer lesson waiting to be learned, and it starts with the verse quoted by Jesus from Hosea: *"I desire mercy, not sacrifice."*

Jesus told the Pharisees: *"If you understood what these words mean. . . ."* Well, what do they mean? Mercy trumps sacrifice. Compassion trumps sin. The Pharisees clung so tightly to their "truth" that they failed to recognize need. Their strict adherence to the law served as blinders to the suffering of those around them. We cannot and must not hold our truth so tightly that we dismiss how valuable another human being is to God.

Through these two vignettes, Jesus suggests that we cannot place every jot and tittle of scripture over our call to serve, care for and forgive. Feed the hungry. Tend to the infirmed.

Think about it. Jesus didn't dishonor the Sabbath. He spent each Sunday in the synagogue. (If you don't see the irony of that statement, maybe that's the problem.) Jesus set aside the Sabbath as a day of worship to God the Father. It was as natural to him as breathing, but not if it meant ignoring a need.

We tend to cherry pick our Sabbaths. Take things out of context without applying the whole of Jesus' teachings. We cannot condone sin, but we are also unqualified to judge it.

Jesus met a woman caught in the act of adultery by another group of Pharisees. Jesus asked them to reflect upon their own sin. When her accusers faded away in the reality of Jesus' question, he told her, *"Neither do I condemn you. . .go and sin no more."* Rather than exclude, Jesus chose to love and teach.

Is it possible that the social issues of our day have become our Sabbath law? The eating of the grain. The man with the shriveled hand. Depending on your personal beliefs, consider them the ancient equivalent of our attitudes toward whomever we deem undesirable.

The Liberal.
The Conservative.
The Gay.
The Transgender.
The Straight.
The Black.

The White.
The Brown.
The Rich.
The Poor.
The Gun Owner.
The Unarmed.

Consider them anyone on whom we pass judgment. Anyone we point to in disdain while channeling our inner Pharisee.

Those in the eyes of whom we easily see the sawdust while disregarding the 2x4 jutting from our own. Judgment is the easy way. Loving is the hard way.

If we are to live as the image of God, if we are to be like Christ, we cannot declare our "truth" or value "being right" more than we value lifting our hands to help the broken, the hurting or the drifting. As soon as we do so, we lose the heart and spirit. . .the image. . .of Jesus. For him, it was always truth and right grounded in love. But always love.

In the story, the Pharisees never see themselves as a tattered robe in need of repair. They see themselves as a garment already cleansed by their strict obedience to the law. . .in need of nothing else. . .now or ever.

Here's the really sad thing about these stories. The Pharisees never doubted that Jesus could heal the man. They begged him to do it. Knew he would. They recognized in him God's sufficient power and gift of healing. They never questioned his ability to heal, only his timing that broke a rule they created to set them apart from others. Staring them in the face was the Son of God, and they could not comprehend.

Never doubt for a moment that God loves the Liberal and Conservative. The Gay. The Transgender. The Straight. The Black. The White. The Brown. The Rich. The Poor. The Gun Owner. The Unarmed. Let us escape the confinement of our entrenched Pharisaical truths.

Jesus calls us to love. Jesus calls us to serve. This week, let's reach out to the hungry heart and the shriveled soul. It is always lawful to do good.

A LIFE OF COMPLETE DEVOTION

Background Passages:
Luke 9:57-62; Philippians 3:12-14

The big day had finally come. To a young boy growing up in the 1960s on a West Texas cotton farm, each day brought a series of chores to be done. Most were routine and boring. Those I deemed "exciting," like jumping on the tractor and plowing the field, were privileges of age and responsibility.

When he deemed me old enough and responsible enough, my Dad entrusted me with an old, yellow Case 400 tractor and a plow called the "lister." We used the lister to prepare the fields for planting. By tilling the soil, we cleared the field of weeds and old stalks and built the furrows and beds necessary for planting.

Hoeing the field, slopping the hogs, moving the irrigation pipe were mind-numbing tasks. Driving the tractor stood as a rite of passage. . .at least it was for this 12-year-old boy. Listing was one of the first "real jobs" my Dad assigned me as I was growing up, "real" being defined as anything involving a tractor and plow. I remember burying my excitement in a cover of feigned indifference. Inside, I was pumped.

As I drove the tractor to my assigned field, Dad followed in his dusty Dodge pick-up. When we arrived, he jumped from the truck and showed me where he wanted me to begin. He explained the hydraulics and showed me how to drop the disk to mark the next row. Dad set the disk and drove the first few rows, straight as an arrow, with me riding along watching. . .a "do as I do" moment.

Listing was one of the first steps in the annual farming process. The planter followed the rows created by the lister. The cultivator followed the planter as the cotton grew to remove weeds and mix and incorporate the soil to ensure that the growing crop had enough water and nutrients to grow well. So if the rows created by the lister were not straight, it made the field difficult to work.

I should note that the rows my Dad plowed as my template looked as if they were drawn with a ruler. Straight as an arrow stretching a quarter mile across our West Texas farm. He had a knack for it.

The task appeared simple to me. Align the front wheel of the tractor with the line drawn by the disk and my rows would be as straight as Dad's. As he climbed off the tractor and bounded toward his truck, he told me before leaving me alone to my work to concentrate on the line ahead of me and "don't look back."

Looking behind you as you plowed was the surest way of getting off line. I scoffed inwardly at Dad's advice. How hard could it be to drive in a straight line?

It turns out that laying that perfect row requires concentration a 12-year-old boy finds difficult to maintain. I remember spending a great deal of time looking behind me, checking on my progress. Every wiggle I saw heightened my anxiety about the quality of my work, compelling me to look time and time again where I had travelled.

The more I worried about it, the worse it looked. My quarter-mile rows meandered through that red soil like a copperhead snake. Dad laughed when he saw it. I eventually learned the lesson he had taught, though I was never quite as good as he was.

God reminded me of that moment in my childhood as I read a passage in the Gospel of Luke. It seems Dad's lesson about farming was as old as the Bible and applies just as neatly to life.

The crowd that followed Jesus generally included his closest disciples and others whose hearts were captured by Jesus' message and ministry. They professed a faith in him and a desire to follow wherever he led them. As the 12 disciples discovered, the requirements of discipleship must be wholeheartedly embraced if we are to live to the fullest the life he wills for us.

The message that day
had not missed its mark.

The words Jesus spoke about God's desire for a relationship

with his people fell on receptive ears.
Hearts were opened.
Lives were changed.

Jesus' call to "follow him"
touched many who came to understand him for who he was.
It instilled in others a desire to do more.

As Jesus left the small village,
he was surrounded by a new group of believers.
Excited.
Eager.
At one point,
a young man touched Jesus' arm.
A conversation of gratitude.
An excited promise.
"I will follow you wherever you go!"

Jesus spoke of the hardship ahead.
No place to lay your head.
No place to call home.
"If you're willing to accept those conditions. . ."
The man.
Unable to commit to such rigors,
walked away.

Jesus turned to another,
a witness to the first exchange.
Sensed his desire to join with Jesus.
"Follow me."
Hesitation.
Indecision.

Written all over his face.
"First, let me go bury my father. . ."
as he turned and walked away.

A third man offered his own pledge.
"I will follow you, Lord.
But first let me go back and say goodbye to my family."

Jesus' eyes revealed his disappointment.
Such promise.
Such potential.
Shaken by circumstance.
Unable to commit.
Jesus offered a resigned response to the reluctant.
"No one who puts his hand to the plow
and looks back is fit for
service in the kingdom of God."

The third man provoked a harsh response from Jesus. This man promised to follow Jesus but asked for time to say goodbye to those he loved, his heart divided between his desire to do as God asked and his love for his family and friends.

Jesus needed these men to think seriously about the commitment they were making. Jesus had "no home, no place to lay his head." Following him meant a life of sacrifice and uncertainty. Jesus wanted more from them than an ill-considered impulse decision that circumstances would make hard to sustain. Count the cost, Jesus suggested, before making a snap decision.

Though willing, the men felt torn between the needs of their families and the responsibilities of discipleship. Jesus told them to get their priorities straight. God's call requires complete devotion to God.

The Greek words translated as *"looks back"* paint a picture of one constantly and continuously looking back at what is left behind. A picture of someone reluctant to let go of the things of the world rather than fully committing his or her life to God. The more we look back, the more likely we are to walk a wavering line of faith life that constantly strays from the path God intends for us.

The lesson for those of us who follow Christ emerges clearly in the conversation Jesus had with the three would-be followers. We must give ourselves completely to the call of Christ by counting and embracing the cost of discipleship and making God's work the most important thing in our life.

Following Christ is never easy, but doing so in a fractured world that demeans and diminishes faith grows ever more difficult. It is made harder when important things in life pull and tug at us from every direction. We must follow Christ despite the hardships, heavy hearts and home ties that block us from giving ourselves completely to him.

God calls us to put our hands on the plow and get on with the work of faith, creating a straight row that makes it easier for him to accomplish his future work. Human nature and the subtle work of a tempter compel us to look back upon the mistakes we've made, those sins in our lives that seek to convince us that God cannot possibly use such a flawed vessel.

Certainly, it may be good to glance behind us on occasion, to revisit our mistakes, as a reminder of how easy it is to fail God. Yet, to dwell in the misery of our past failures inhibits our ability to be useful in service ministry, makes us feel unworthy of the purpose to which we have been called.

Just as troubling are those times when we think wistfully of the "good ol' days" when life and faith were easier. Today is the time we have been given. Looking back and wishing the world were different prohibits us from seeing in front of us the God-directed opportunities that allow us to demonstrate his love for a world that can no longer plow a straight row.

Don't look back, Christ says. Give yourself wholly to your call and count the cost. Christ cannot accept our conditional or half-hearted service. Nor can we spend time looking back at our past, reveling in a simpler time or lamenting our failures.

He asks us instead to look forward; to press on. To open ourselves to the possibilities of service and ministry.

Paul captured the same message in his letter to the Philippian church as he declared that he could not fully grasp all that God called him to be. *"Brothers, I do not consider myself to have embraced it yet. But this one thing I do: Forgetting what lies behind and straining forward to what lies ahead, I press on. . . ."*

Experience is a great teacher. I eventually learned to rely on that handy, pivoting disk on the plow that I raised and lowered as I traversed the field. If I kept my eyes fixed on the line as it ran into the distance, put my tractor wheel in its small furrow and followed it to the end, my rows rarely wavered.

For those committed to Christ, for those who wish to live as his mirrored image, Jesus drew the line in the sand with his life as the perfect example to follow. Most of us recognize that our line drifts away from the line Jesus walked. Our mistakes compound when we spend too much time looking behind us.

Let's keep our eyes focused constantly on him and the path of righteousness he walked as an example to all of us. I promise it will make life that much easier to plow.

A LIFE OF DISCIPLINE IN THE FACE OF TEMPTATION

Background Passages:
Matthew 4:1-11; Luke 4:1-13

He stood on the high bank
on the east side of the Jordan River.
Looked down at the milling masses
lining up to be baptized by John.

The butterflies in Jesus' stomach fluttered,
the stirring of the Holy Spirit within.
For the past 18 years he had waited.
Listening for God's call
to begin the work he was sent to do.
"It's time, Jesus."
The voice within urges him on.

Jesus shuffled forward in the meandering line.
Waited his turn.
Deep in thought.
His sandals sank into the mud.
Toes touched water.

Snapping back to reality,
he looked into the disbelieving eyes of his cousin
staring back at him.
"Why are you here?"
"I am not worthy. . . ."
"You should baptize me. . . ."
"No, John, you need to do this for me. . .

I need you to do this for me."

As he rose from the cool waters of the Jordan,
liquid cascaded from his hair and beard.
Jesus wiped the water from his eyes.
Looked to heaven.
A prayer on his lips.

The clouds broke.
A dove descended.
A voice declared his name. . . .
"My Son. . . ."
Value.
Validation.
A mountaintop experience on the
floor of a river valley.

Jesus slogged out of the river.
Climbed the bank.
Retraced his steps to the crest of the hill.
Jesus looked back at the crowd below,
waiting for their shot at redemption.
Unaware that redemption had
stood among them.

He turned away from his past.
Took one step into the
jagged edge of the wilderness.
Another
and another.
Into the desert
to face the life options open to him.

*****

Every step Jesus took into the barren, desolate and deserted landscape led him to a familiar place. I doubt it was his first time in the solitude of the wilderness.

A place to ponder.
A place to plan.
A place to pray.

Led by the Spirit as if the Father called to his son: "Let's go someplace where we can talk."

In the weeks after the spiritual high of his baptism, he found himself sitting in the shade of a hollow carved into the desert rock by wind and rain, looking back toward the setting sun over Judea. . .in the direction of Jerusalem, where he knew his path would someday take him to the cross.

We call it the "Temptations of Christ" as if this was the first time Jesus faced his own human desires. We want our savior to be immune to the pressure of living up to God's expectations. As God's son, we want Jesus to have known from the moment he was born what his role would be and how it would play out. We don't think of him tempted as a young boy to lash out in selfish anger. Tempted as a teenager to disobey his mother's command. Tempted as a man to stay with the family business rather than take that journey to Jerusalem.

We want to think that Jesus never faced the choices we face. Never faced the litany of options that pull us from God's will. We want Jesus to have demonstrated his rock-solid faith and obedience to God from the moment of his birth until he rose again into heaven.

To lock Jesus in that box of spiritual piety puts him on a heavenly leash, restrained from the possibility of sin. Negating the free will God gave him. Taking those possibilities from him makes his human birth unnecessary. His walk among us a sham. If the cross was not a choice, his ultimate sacrifice loses its meaning.

When Jesus walked into the wilderness, ready to begin his ministry, he faced a world of choices that would determine if he would follow the will of his Father or chart his own course. It was a time for Jesus to prepare himself mentally, emotionally and spiritually for the life ahead. He had to decide what kind of Messiah he would be. The Messiah God sent him to be or the one for whom the people would later clamor.

After weeks of prayer and preparation in the desert during which all these possibilities flashed through his mind, Jesus awakens to his ravishing hunger. A voice begins picking at the heart of Jesus, trying to shake his resolve. The stone looks a lot like a biscuit. The voice says, "You're hungry. To do this work, you've got to take care of yourself. Under the circumstances, no one would blame you if you were a little self-absorbed. Just say the word. . . ." Jesus knew the power given to him by the Father. The counterargument of sin pushed him to selfishly abuse his God-given power. To place his own desires first in his life.

Yet, Jesus understood that selfishness served as a stumbling block to service and sacrifice. *"Man shall not live by bread alone. . . ."* The work of God is not about us. It's about those who need God's touch in their lives. Living in the image of God demands that we set aside the selfish desires of our hearts and mirror the heart of God.

The voice in his heart says, "God will protect you in all circumstances. Hurl yourself from the temple roof. When the people see that you land unharmed, you will draw a crowd. Then when you preach, they will have to believe." Jesus understood that we cannot bend God's will to ours. We cannot force his hand by insisting our way is better.

Jesus knew that calling attention to himself by an ostentatious show of power might attract a crowd, but the faith it bought could not be sustained. *"Do not test the Lord, your God. . . ."* His plan for our lives remains the perfect plan. Our errant decisions derail what God intended for us. We must avoid dictating the terms of our obedience to a God who knows us better than we know ourselves.

Jesus hears the voice say, "You've been asked to do the impossible. It doesn't have to be that hard. I can set you up as ruler of the world with a snap of my fingers. Bow down to me. I'll make it happen. No drama. No trauma. No painful sacrifice. Kneel."

Jesus fought the urge to take the easy road. It may have been a daily struggle throughout his ministry. As he began to grasp the magnitude of the sacrifice God asked of him, at a time when he could only imagine the agony that would come, he resisted sin's easy path in favor of the road less traveled.

He chose to connect with the one who offered real power rather than the one whose power was limited. *"Get behind me, Satan. Worship the Lord your God and serve him only. . . ."*

To be sure, Jesus faced tough choices in the wilderness. We want the temptations of Christ to have ended in the wilderness, but they didn't. Throughout his life on earth, Jesus faced the choice to do things differently. . .right up until the end.

Sitting alone in the darkness of Gethsemane, agonizing over that which he knew lay ahead, Jesus fell to his knees. The depth of anguish evident as the prayer he prayed to his God poured from his heart. *"Please, take this cup from me. If there is any other way to do this, let's find it."* When the voice inside him remained silent, he knew God's way was the only way to bring salvation to a lost world. *"Not my will, but yours be done."*

A temptation.

A choice.

A decision.

If our strength to face the temptations we encounter feels weak in comparison to Jesus' resolve, it is only because our connection to the one who gives that strength is frayed by our own selfish desires. We see it when we try to bend God's will to serve our purpose. When we choose to follow the path of rebellion. . .the easy road. . .rather than rely on the power of God to keep us from stumbling on the rocks along the road he asks us to travel.

Will I live life my way or God's way? Will I love or reject? Will I serve or demand? Will I help or hurt? Will I give or covet? The decisions we make must reflect his will and not ours. To live in the image of God requires us to make an active decision to do so. Every day. Every minute. With every decision point.

Sin will promise the world. God gives us the freedom to follow or flee. We do, or we don't. To live as the image of God in a world pushing us toward bad choices, we must meet every temptation as Jesus did.

A temptation.

A choice.

A decision.

Which will it be?

A LIFE OF SERVICE ABOVE SELF

Background Passage:
Matthew 14:9-23

No physical pain eclipses the pain of losing a close friend or family member. The grief of personal loss hurts. Shatters our sense of normalcy. Threatens our emotional stability. Chokes the very breath from our souls.

Grief may be tempered by the circumstances of our loss. When a loved one has faced months of pain from an insidious disease, for instance, the believer feels a sense of comfort and release knowing that a mother, a sister or a friend is no longer suffering. That realization may lessen the gravity on a sad heart, but it does little to fill the emptiness one feels.

Grief is a process, as anyone who has lived it knows. Our reactions to it are as individual as our own unique personalities.

In their respected book, *On Death and Dying*, Elizabeth Kubler-Ross and David Kessler plotted the five stages of grief through which all must pass. People express themselves differently and may well maneuver through the stages in a different way or at a different pace, but the authors suggest that we must pass through each stage if we are to recover from the grief that engulfs us following the loss of someone special to us.

Kubler-Ross and Kessler define the stages of grief: Denial. . .a time of shock and emotional paralysis when we tend to avoid our new reality. Anger. . .a time when all the emotions we bottled up for a time get released. Bargaining. . .when we look for alternatives to fill the void within us. Depression. . .when reality weighs us down. Acceptance. . .finding our way forward into a new normal.

I know two families going through the death of a family member this week. Having walked in their shoes with my own family and wanting to offer some word of comfort, I found myself scanning the scripture that might grant all of us a foothold on the slippery slope of sorrow.

The well-meaning will offer these families suggestions in the coming days based on their personal experiences. I suspect the intent will be appreciated, but the words will have limited effect. The path through the stages is unique to each individual because we are unique and our relationship to the one who died was unique to us.

We are not alone in our sorrow. Scripture tells us that Jesus was familiar with sorrow and suffering caused by the death of someone for whom he cared deeply. However, I suspect there were a thousand occasions when Jesus put his arm around a crying widow, offered a prayer for a brother in mourning, took a meal to a neighbor who lost a sister, prayed for a family whose mother died peacefully in her sleep or stood quietly beside a parent whose child was ravaged by disease when no word would bring comfort.

His experiences with grief were not second hand. Jesus on earth was not spared the emotional trauma death brings. Late in his earthly ministry, his good friend Lazarus died. Though Jesus knew the outcome of this experience, scripture tells us he wept. His anguish over the loss of someone he loved was real and heart-wrenching.

Yet, another profound encounter with death touched Jesus at the beginning of his ministry. Not too long after Jesus gathered his disciples together and taught them things they needed to know about the kingdom of God, he sent them out, two-by-two, on a mission trip to preach the good news of God's coming salvation.

At the same time, Herod, the Judean tetrarch, fearful of a popular uprising, arrested John the Baptist, Jesus' cousin and early partner in ministry. The Baptist ran afoul of the regional governor when he challenged Herod's divorce and marriage to his sister. While John was in prison, Herod, intrigued by his step-daughter, promised her anything she wished. After talking to her conniving mother, the step-daughter asked for John the Baptist's head on a platter. Herod did not disappoint and ordered John beheaded.

News of this horrific death reached Jesus just as the disciples were returning from their trip. The news was unsettling. The two men, connected by circumstance of birth and passion of ministry, held deep respect for each other.

Jesus once told the crowds who followed him that *"among those born of women there is none greater than John,"* revealing his level of affection and respect for the tough-minded preacher. Jesus' love was returned many times over. John stood waist-deep in the Jordan when Jesus presented himself to be baptized at the start of his earthly ministry. Knowing who he was and the nature of his work, John hesitated.

"I'm not worthy to tie your sandals," he said.

So when Jesus heard the news about his cousin, Matthew 14 tells us that *". . .he withdrew by boat privately to a solitary place."*

Saddened.
Distraught.

Struggling with both the personal loss and the method of execution. Seeing in John's death, perhaps, a reflection of his own future.

As he so often did when troubled with life, Jesus needed to feel the presence of his heavenly father. In the middle of the excitement of the missionary reports, he moved away from the crowd to find a quiet place to be alone in his thoughts, to deal with his emotions and his grief.

Yet the crowd wouldn't let him. Maybe they were unaware of John's death. Maybe they didn't understand the connection between the men as cousins. Maybe they were so caught up in their own struggles they couldn't see into the hurting heart of another person. Whatever possessed them to come, a large crowd circled around the Sea of Galilee to wait as Jesus' boat came ashore.

Many of us can empathize with Jesus. He needed his time alone. . .his space to deal with his own emotions. Life would not allow it. Jesus had a choice: to look inward or outward. We face the same choice in times like this. We can turn inside ourselves, skirt the crowd and run into the desert alone. Or we can look outside ourselves to the people pressing around us and have "compassion on them."

Matthew tells us that Jesus saw the crowd and *"had compassion on them."* What an amazing picture this presents! A grieving Christ greets the gathering crowd.

When most of us would turned the boat around, Jesus dried his tear-stained cheeks with the sleeve of his cloak, said a new prayer for emotional strength, took in a deep breath and went about his work healing the sick and comforting the sorrowful.

He spent the rest of the day with them, eventually feeding them with a little bread and fish before sending them on their way. A picture settles in my thoughts. The last family finally turned to leave. Jesus, who set aside his own sorrow for that time, waited until they were out of sight before plopping heavily on a boulder and allowing the emotion pent inside to flow freely. Scripture says that at some point he gathered himself, climbed the mountain behind him as he had intended to do earlier that day, seeking refuge in a father who understood clearly the heaviness in his heart.

So, what does this tell me about grief? Based on my own experience, it may well tell me what I already know. My faith pales in comparison to the faith of Jesus. I think this biblical episode tells us life never stops.

Never slows down.

Never considers your emotional state.

Life goes on.

The daze of days surrounding the loss of a loved one blows by with little regard to what we want or need to do. In the days that follow death, there will be bills to pay. Places to go where no one knows our anguish. Children tugging at our sleeve who need us to be in the moment with them. Co-workers expecting us to be on our game. Work still to be done. Our ability to find the peace we need, the solitude we crave, gets overshadowed by the press of the crowd around us.

We can push the crowd away or do as Jesus did when he pulled the boat to shore. . .embrace for a moment the opportunity God puts in front of us to serve him. To testify through our last reserve of faith and strength to the power of the father who gives us the ability to put one foot in front of the other. To move ashore when all we want to do is turn the boat around.

I don't want to minimize the difficulty of the grief walk we all must take. It is healthy to grieve. Healthy to find time alone to consider the meaning of this personal loss. Healthy to weep. Grief unfolds before us in a variable timeline as a path of ministry. As Jesus sailed the boat across the Sea of Galilee that day, I suspect the horizon lay unseen in the distance, obscured by the tears in his eyes. His vision limited to the prow of the boat as he stared blankly into a tomorrow without his dear friend. That's the way I feel on days like that.

However deeply Jesus mourned John's death, he didn't stay in the boat. He turned grief into the fuel that fired his own sense of mercy and ministry. You see, all the hurt and pain we experience after the death of a loved one can empower us to love more deeply and to serve more willingly.

These two friends of mine who mourn this week the loss of a brother and sister, respectively, will be in Collique, Peru next week on a mission trip, building small homes for families who possess next to nothing. Despite their personal sorrow, they will step out of their boats on the shore of a dusty hill in South America to share the compassion of Christ with strangers unaware of the grief they bear. That, my friends, is living in the image of God.

In our most desperate times, our dependence on Jesus Christ serves as a dynamic testimony to this lost and dying world. It is okay to grieve. It's is okay to cry. It's good to mourn for lost loved ones, but may our emotions turn ever outward to spirit-inspired, Gospel-driven compassion.

A LIFE OF SPIRITUAL INFLUENCE

Background Passages:
Luke 1: 26-38; Luke 1:46-55; Luke 2:22-40;
John 2:1-12; John 19:25-27

Mother's Day lies just around the corner. I'm reminded of words spoken by the late Dr. Billy Graham on the unique opportunity God gives women to influence and impact the lives of others in ways that few men can.

"There is nothing in this world more personal, as nurturing or as life-changing, as the influence of a righteous woman."

Don't get me wrong; I'm not minimizing the man's role in God's world. When men allow God to rule their lives and women live out their call to righteous living, there is a divine balance that makes the world a better place.

However, as most of us blessed with wonderful mothers can testify, Dr. Graham's statement rings with the peal of abiding truth. I have felt it in my own life. The righteous influence of godly women. . .a wife, a mother, aunts, Sunday school teachers, public school teachers and countless friends. .

.absolutely shaped and molded who I am, spiritually, professionally and personally. A new generation of women led by my two amazing daughters-in-law continues to teach me the things I need to know about being the man God needs me to be every day.

As I think of the women who influenced my life, I realize how blessed I am to have known so many women who believed in me. Women who supported me. Women who propped me up when I stood on the edge of failure. I think of the women who lifted me up at some point in my life with their presence. . .their words. . .their friendship. . .their touch. . .just when I needed to hear or feel it. Their influence is a tremendous gift in my life!

I'm convinced God placed these women in my life for a reason. Their influence in my life shifted from piddling to powerful because they live each day as righteous women.

So what does it mean to be a righteous woman of influence?

Of all the women of influence in the Bible, I point you to Mary, the mother of Jesus. We Baptists fail to give Mary the credit she deserves for her unrecognized impact on Jesus' life. Mary wasn't perfect. She didn't walk around with a halo above her head. She was certainly more than a simple vessel God used to carry his Son. To better understand Mary's role, embrace the humanity of Jesus.

Let me explain. We tend to think of Jesus in the divine. We casually recognize his humanity, but we want to color it heavily with his godliness. We like to think Jesus was pulled from the womb without crying, speaking King James English and turning water into milk.

We don't think of him as a baby with colic, crying through the night. A toddler who fell and bumped his head on the table Joseph built. A three-year-old disciplined for taking a toy from his little brother. We don't think of him as a little boy scraping his knee while chasing a friend. As a teenager who thought the little Jewish girl down the street was pretty. We never consider that as a young apprentice carpenter, he one day bashed his thumb with a hammer, biting back the ugly word you and I might say.

If he came into the world to be like us, we have to embrace his human side. . .acknowledge the perfect way he dealt with all those very human situations. If we can fully accept Jesus' humanity, that part of his personhood had a very human mother. . .one amazingly normal, human mother.

The mother who lost it at times because she was up three nights in a row with a squalling baby. The mother who swatted the hand of a three-year-old for taking his brother's toy. The mother who looked at that pretty little Jewish girl as a threat to her son. The mother who kissed the scraped knees and laughed at her son when he swallowed that ugly word after bashing his thumb.

If Mary was an ordinary, very human woman, why did God choose her to be the mother of his only begotten son? Why was she so *"highly favored?"*

I think God chose Mary because he knew the person she was. Knew the kind of mother she would be. God chose Mary because he knew she would love Jesus unconditionally. Knew she would teach him about life and model everything good in it. God chose Mary because she would stand beside him in the darkest hours of his life. He chose Mary above all others because she possessed a mother's instinct to raise Jesus with the spiritual and moral integrity to tackle the mission God planned for him as the savior of the world.

God chose Mary because she lived as a righteous woman of influence.

Mary's story begins in bizarre fashion. Not every woman could handle the news she heard. Mary possessed the spiritual depth to believe an implausible message.

It is one thing to accept the unlikely future while the angel speaks. It's another thing to stay faithful when the angel disappears into the darkness. The rational side of Mary knew her pregnancy would bring a host of life-altering issues. . .

> . . .ridicule and disgrace. . .
> . . .embarrassment to her family. . .
> . . .Joseph's anger.

What strikes me most about Mary's response to the unexpected visit from the angel is that, in the end, she submitted to the will of God with such obedience and trust. She said in response to all she heard,

"May it be to me as you have said."

What an amazing moment of faith and obedience! Despite knowing the difficulties this decision posed in her life, she allowed God to work his will. How often do you think Jesus heard this story as he was growing up? Imagine the lesson of obedience and faith it taught him.

Still, like the disciples and like us, Mary struggled to understand God's way of working through his redemptive plan. Her understanding of "Messiah" did not include a tragic death. Though she heard it in the temple when Jesus was born, she did not anticipate that a *"sword would pierce her soul."* Even though she didn't have Jesus all figured out, she grappled with the unknown, trusted God and remained faithful to his call in her life.

More than once we see when Mary *"pondered in her heart"* all that happened around her. She did more than simply deliberate the meaning of a word or event. Rather, she watched, listened and thought about all that happened around her and her son in light of the message from the angel that night, in light of the words from the rabbi and prophetess in the temple.

She constantly made connections, determining how she could help make God's plan come to pass in the life of her son. Not content to just let life happen, she laid the groundwork needed to bring it to pass.

At some point in Jesus' life, Mary's faith, obedience and trust stood out as an encouragement to Jesus when he was struggling to follow God's plan. Can't you almost hear Mary's words whispered in the Garden of Gethsemane as Jesus agonized over his impending death on the cross?

I believe that at such a time, Jesus recalled the words of his mother when she told the angel *"May it be to me as you said."* His prayer says *"Not my will, but yours. . .,"* the essence of obedience and trust. . .Mary's model of faith that carried him through his most difficult times.

To be a woman of influence requires obedience to God and trust in his plan for your life.

We encounter Mary again in scripture when she visits her aunt, Elizabeth. After they share their miraculous stories of God's blessing, Mary sings a song from her heart. Find in the words of Mary's song the boldness to call for God's justice in an oppressive, unjust world. Find in Mary's song the words and deeds of Jesus. She sings from Old Testament scripture the traits of a living God:

". . .you are mindful of me in my humble state. . . ." Look at Jesus' own humility before God.

". . .scatters the proud. . . ." Look at Jesus' challenge to the ritualistic faith of the Pharisees.

". . .lifts up the humble. . . ." Look at how Jesus worked so fervently for the poor and needy.

". . .fills the hungry. . . ." Look at how Jesus fed the multitudes both physically and spiritually.

". . .he is merciful. . . ." Look at how Jesus offered mercy to those who did not deserve it.

This was the image of God that Mary carried in her heart. Things she learned from scripture even before the culture really allowed women to study God's word. She internalized the scripture she read or heard to the point where it shaped her life and ultimately the life of Jesus. That was the God she knew. That was the character of God she taught God's son.

I can imagine Mary singing her song to Jesus every night as she laid him in bed as a child, a poignant lullaby. . .embedding those godly virtues into his very being. Modeling it for him every day. In the end, her influence contributed to his role as the servant Messiah.

To be a righteous woman of influence, ground yourself in scripture. Let it guide your actions. Share its meaning with those you love. Live out its lessons as you tend to the needs of others.

We see Mary again at the wedding in Cana. She tried to work through a potentially embarrassing situation when the host family ran out of wine. She brought the problem to Jesus.

Why would she do that? Jesus even asked her, *"Why are you bothering me with this? My time has not come."*

My mind sees Mary looking deeply into the eyes of Jesus without saying a word. Never taking her eyes off his, she spoke to the servant beside her, *"Do whatever he says to do."* The twinkle in her eye and the crooked smile on her face signaled her belief that Jesus would do the right thing. . .every time. Her trust in him full and complete.

Perhaps that one look gave Jesus permission to be who he was intended to be. It is as if she were saying, "Now is as good a time as any, my son. I don't need you as much as the world needs you. What are you waiting for?"

A woman becomes a righteous woman of influence by playing the role she plays. . .recognizing when it's time to push the bird from the nest. Knowing when a simple word of encouragement to someone will convince them it is time to get started doing what God called them to do. . .time to take that leap of faith. Letting them know, "This is your time."

The most endearing and enduring passage concerning Mary takes place at the foot of the cross. Scripture paints a vivid picture of a mother watching the son she raised and loved dying an agonizing death on the cross. A death she could not comprehend. Only a mother who has lost a child can begin to fathom the emotional suffering Mary experienced as she heard his ragged breathing. Saw the pain etched on his features. Watched his life flow out with every drop of blood spilled on that rocky soil.

The words Jesus whispered from the cross to John and Mary tell us everything about Mary's influence on Jesus.

> *"Behold your Mother."*
> "Behold your son."

Jesus loved his mother so deeply he could not let death take him without ensuring that Mary would never be alone. Jesus recognized through his own pain the deep sorrow of one who loved him. Surely, while on that cross, there were flashbacks to every embrace, every kiss, every smile.

Jesus hung on that cross, feeling like God had abandoned him, looking down on a mother who never could. A mother whose love was endless.

You become a righteous woman of influence when you love others so deeply that you are deeply loved in return.

My mom passed away in 1998. I cannot explain the magnitude of her impact on my life. . .

. . .my understanding of who I am. . .

. . .how I relate to others. . .

. . .the focus and purpose of my life.

I learned from her delightfully sarcastic sense of humor. Never mean-spirited, but always catching you off guard. She taught me that life needs laughter and that it was always easiest to laugh at yourself, if for no other reason than to avoid taking yourself too seriously.

She taught me to deeply respect the ability of women to be accomplished in any field, reminding me to keep capable, intelligent and independent women in my life. I loved it when she convinced my sister to leave the nursing field and become a medical doctor because she was smarter than most men with the degree.

She instilled in me an understanding that marriage was a partnership, promising to break my arm if she ever heard that I did not help with the housework.

She taught me about being a beloved grandparent. I loved how every minute she spent with our kids was personal and filled with joy. She was, after all, the one who sat on the floor with my boys and their cousins and taught them to play poker.

Like Mary, my mom was obedient to her God, trusting him in all areas of life. Demonstrating her faith in the most difficult of times. She was able to do so because she was grounded in and guided by scripture, knowing just how to apply Christ's teaching in the most practical of ways.

Mom encouraged each of her children to pursue our dreams and passions, instilling in us the belief that we could do anything. There were times when she pushed us with an impeccable sense of timing to start down the path God intended for us.

In the end, Mom was loved deeply because she deeply loved.

You see it, don't you? Living in the image of God has nothing to do with gender and everything to do with godliness.

Without a doubt, like Mary, my mom was one of those righteous women of influence.

A LIFE OF FORGIVENESS

Background Passage:
Matthew 18:21-35

One can't be sure what prompted the question. Perhaps it was born out of a natural argument among men who traveled together days on end. Men getting on each other's nerves after too much time together, staring into the distance from opposite sides of the road.

Perhaps the question popped into his head after hearing another rabbi expound in heavy monotone in the local synagogue about the law's limit on human forgiveness.

Perhaps the question rattled around his brain after hearing Jesus teach about harmony among believers and dealing with the unrepentant sinner among them.

Whatever the prompt, Peter sidled up to Jesus one day with an honest question about forgiveness. *"How many times shall I forgive my brother or sister who sins against me?"*

The Jewish law Peter knew laid specific guidelines for forgiveness, declaring that you should forgive anyone three times. One was not obligated to forgive a fourth offense. The question Peter posed reflected the thinking of the day. Surely, there is a point at which forgiveness is no longer expected. In essence, "When can I stop forgiving someone who hurts me?"

His follow up question suggests that Peter had a gut feeling that Jesus always lived in a "walk-the-extra-mile, turn-the-other-cheek" kind of world when it came to the law. He certainly saw evidence of Jesus' boundless forgiveness in his time with his Lord. So Peter exerted his opinion in the form of another question. *"How many times shall I forgive a brother or sister who sins against me? Seven times?"*

In the debate bouncing around in his head, Peter must have thought he would catch an "atta boy" from his Master for his magnanimous spirit. "The law says 'three times.' Let's double that and add one for good measure. Now that's turning the other cheek."

Maybe it played out like this:

Jesus stooped as he walked
down the dusty path.
Picking up a chunk of gray basalt
along the side of the road.
"That's a great question, Peter."
Jesus bounced the rock in his hand a time or two.
Thinking about his response.
Casually threw the rock side-armed.
Bouncing it off the trunk of a cypress tree
60 feet down the road.

"I tell you, Peter.

It's more than that.
You're still too literal. Not seven times.
Seventy-seven times.
"We won't get through this life
without someone hurting us.
Taking advantage.
Offending.
Insulting.
Happens in the closest families.
Happens within the fellowship.

"How much do we damage all those relationships
if we put a limit on our forgiveness?
Doesn't our limited attitude
set a substantial barrier between us and
those we are supposed to love?
"The law says three.
You say seven.
Both are limits."

Jesus sat under the same cypress tree
he had plunked with the stone.
Glad to get out of the summer heat.
His disciples settled around him.
Each took a quick drink from a shared
water bag Nathaniel carried.

No heavy sermon.
No deep theology.
Just a tongue-in cheek story to teach

a powerful lesson about the
size of their hearts.

"The kingdom we're trying to build here is different.
Let's suppose. . . ."

Jesus then launched into a parable about a king to whom a servant owed more money that the disciples could imagine. Ten thousand talents. Historians tell us a talent represented the equivalent of 6,000 days' wages. Staggering! The number Jesus imagined would support a man for 164,000 years.

Hear the laughter roll through the disciples as they could scarcely comprehend the outrageous fortune the man owed. Hyperbole of the highest magnitude. Jesus laughed with them. Sees that he's captured their attention.

Jesus continued. The time came to collect the bill, and the king said, *"Pay up or you and your family will be sold into slavery and all you own will be confiscated to repay what is owed"*. . .knowing full well the servant's assets scarcely made a dent in the debt.

The man fell on the floor promising to repay what he had no hope of repaying. Grasping at straws. Begging for mercy. Yet, somehow, the man's contrite spirit touched the king deeply.

Jesus mimicked wiping a tear from his eyes. *"Your debt is cancelled. Go home."*

The disciples reacted with a chuckle and a few comments about the king's enormous wealth. Jesus waited until they settled down, his playful demeanor turning more solemn.

"Now suppose this very relieved servant. . ."

Jesus' brow furrowed in thought, eyes searching deeply into the heart of each disciple as he speaks. He explained how the forgiven servant encountered a colleague who owed him six months' wages, a pittance compared with his former debt Yet, the man whose debt was wiped clean grabbed his friend by the scruff of the neck demanding his payment.

That servant was in no better place financially than the forgiven one. Using the exact same words the first servant spoke to the king, the man fell on the ground. Begged for mercy. Promised to pay back a difficult, but not impossible, sum of money. Rather than extend the same mercy he received, the man had the other thrown in jail until his debt could be paid.

The injustice described hit home with the disciples. Caught up in the story, they grumbled a bit, angry at the first servant.

Jesus became more animated as he continued the parable, his words coming more rapidly. *"Now, when the king found out, he was livid and called the first servant before him. You wicked servant! I canceled all your debt because you begged me. Where is your mercy toward the one who owed you?"*

The disciples pondered the words during the pregnant silence that hung in the air like a morning mist. Jesus added *"This is how my Father will treat you unless you forgive your brother and sister from your heart."*

I think Jesus liked Peter's question. It gave him a chance to help the disciples sink the plow of personal belief a little more deeply into the fertile soil of faith. It never crossed Jesus' mind to make forgiveness a quantifiable event. Yet the religious law of the day did exactly that. Dragging the plow along the surface, setting the standard in shallow attitudes, seemed to look forward to a day of retaliation rather than a time of reconciliation.

Peter had stretched the legal limit as far as he felt comfortable. "I know you expect more from us, Jesus, than the law requires." And, in that moment of inspiration, he doubled the law's demand and added one on which to grow. "Seven seems like a fair number," proud of the forbearance it showed.

But Jesus understood forgiveness as a way of being. . .a lifestyle choice. To Jesus, forgiveness was a way of relating to others. Thinking about others. Loving others. Forgiveness is nothing less than the way of Christ. If we are to live in his image, forgiveness must be our way as well. Not three times. Not seven times, but as an open expression of the one to whom we belong.

Picture Jesus. Visiting with the woman at the well, turning her from her troubled lifestyle.

Watch him. Writing in the dirt next to the woman caught in the act of adultery as the Pharisees who wished to stone her walked away with guilt-laden feet. *"Neither do I condemn you. Go and sin no more."*

See him. Wrapping his arm around Peter who lived for weeks with the sound of that rooster crowing in his head. *"Feed my sheep."*

Forgiveness.

The way of Christ.

An infinite, life-altering act of grace.

In his book, *Mere Christianity*, C. S. Lewis wrote, "Forgiveness is a lovely idea, until there is something to forgive." A promising premise, in principle, until we face the dreadful reality of pardoning the grievous and unforgivable.

Our lives are filled with broken promises, bitter betrayals and hurt feelings. We cry over unkind words, licking our physical and emotional wounds, telling our stories of loss and pain at the hands of another. Underneath all of it lies the question of forgiveness. How can we move past the hurt and into the healing?

Jesus told his disciples that forgiveness flows from the heart. He meant that they must dig deeply into their innermost being and find a way to set aside their anger, frustration and bitterness. To offer sincere words of forgiveness wrapped in the warmth of God's love, extended with a handshake or embrace.

If the greatest attribute of God in Christ is love, one could make an argument that forgiveness is the greatest expression of love. This much seems to be true. . .living in the image of God requires us to demonstrate boundless forgiveness. It's not that easy.

I have listened in amazement to a man whose son was the innocent victim of a drive-by shooting talk sincerely about forgiving the one who senselessly took his son's life. I have heard honest words of forgiveness from a woman whose beloved grandmother was killed because the drunk driver shared one too many glasses of wine.

How can we hear testimonies like those and still harbor resentment toward the person who sat in *our* pew last Sunday? How can we let a few ill-chosen words of a neighbor cut us off from the fellowship we once enjoyed?

When we start counting the offenses we suffer at the hands of another. . .adding up the chalk marks until that day when we can say "Enough is enough. . ." then we're living exactly like the first servant in Jesus' story. While we ignore the 10,000 talents of sin our Father forgave us, we hold our offender by the scruff of the neck, demanding payment. . .unwilling to forgive even the slightest of sins against us.

I share breakfast and Bible reading once a week with a group of men in the community in which I work. Every breakfast ends with the Lord's Prayer. The model prayer offers a petition and an expectation: "Forgive us our trespasses as we forgive those who trespass against us."

Jesus said as much to the disciples as he wrapped up this impromptu lesson. I see him rising from the tree under which he sat, bending down to pick up another rock, bouncing in lightly in his hand. He reared back and threw it, striking another bullseye on the trunk of another cypress tree 60 feet farther down the road.

Setting off down the road again, he ended the lesson with a casual but cautionary moral to the story: "If you don't forgive others, how can God possible forgive you?"

The lesson Jesus taught his disciples, he also teaches us. Peter shared our human tendency to limit forgiveness. But to forgive beyond counting is inhuman. It doesn't originate with us. It is born of a heart changed by God through Christ and his indwelling spirit of grace living within us.

Christ living in us.

We, in turn, living in the image of Christ.

A LIFE SPENT THIRSTING FOR RIGHTEOUSNESS

Background Passages:
Luke 2:41-52; Philippians 2:6-7; I Corinthians 3:1-3

I don't know if your family gatherings were like mine growing up. Typically, everyone brought a pot luck casserole or vegetable, while someone provided the ham. Everyone would meet at Grandma's house after church on Sunday. The cousins would play. . .loudly. . .while the food was placed on the dining room table, extended to its full length.

Card tables sat in the "formal" living room, surrounded by those folding chairs that pinched more than one finger at some point during the day. After a prayer, the adults sat around the dining room table, banishing the kids with their paper plates to the card tables in the next room.

I remember listening from the other room to the conversation around the big table. Sometimes it was filled with love and laughter. Sometimes it was serious and somber.

Each of us cousins longed for the day when Grandma would point us to a chair at the big table. What a glorious rite of passage! No longer a child. Now, an adult.

I wonder if Jesus felt that way when he entered the temple in Jerusalem when he was 12 years old. Picture it.

Every year in memory.
The boy had traveled with his family from
Galilee to Jerusalem
to celebrate the Passover.

His father.
Devout and upright.
Walked with his son into the temple,
hand resting lightly on his son's shoulder.

Each year,
the son experienced the awe and majesty
of the towering, white-washed temple stone
glistening in the morning sun.

The father.
Dropped to a knee.
Took the young boy by the shoulders.
Reminded him of his place.
Pointed him to the other children
against the wall. . .
to look,
listen and
learn.
Being seen. Never heard.

With a smile and a gentle push,
Joseph sent Jesus to join the other boys,
all of whom longed for the invitation to sit
among the men.

To learn at the feet of Jerusalem's most noted rabbis.
What a difference this year made!
Jesus.
On the verge of Jewish adulthood,
entered his final year of study.
To become a "son of the covenant."

This, his first year to sit among the men
in the temple in Jerusalem,
a moment about which Jesus had dreamt for years.

This special day,
Jesus stood a little straighter beside his father
just inside the gates of the inner courtyard.
Joseph marveled at the lad.
Now nearly as tall as he.
The young man's eyes fixed straight ahead.
A slight smile on his face.
Anticipating and yearning.

Jesus watched with fond recollection.
His father again took a knee,
hands resting on the shoulders of his younger brothers. . . .
A quiet word.
A gentle push.
Sending them to stand with the other boys.

Joseph.
Watched them walk away.
Brushed the dust from his robe.
Gazed down at his oldest son.
Knowing the importance of the day for Jesus,
he grinned.
He nodded.
The two walked into the gathering crowd of men.
Jesus.
A child standing on the
threshold of adulthood.

The day ended.
The thrill of the conversation
not lost on Jesus.
The rabbi taught and questioned.
Jesus listened.
Never a word uttered.
Never a question asked.
Respectful of the moment.
Taking it all in.

That night, he visited with family.
Excited by the day.
Full of questions left unasked at the temple.

The group of family and friends
rose bright and early the next morning,
setting out on a long journey home. . .
all except Jesus.
He had every intention of returning home.

In the hustle of the morning,
the burning questions in his heart
consumed him.

Without thinking,
he found himself again inside the temple.
Sitting on the steps among the men.
Listening with rapt attention to the words of the rabbi.
No longer overwhelmed by the moment.
Jesus could no longer contain himself.
Listened.
Commented.
Clarified.
Probed.

His questions startled the rabbi.

When the rabbi tried to turn the table,
asked his own questions in return,
Jesus did not shy away.
He thought.
He considered.
He recited passages of scripture supporting his thoughts.

The dialogue intrigued the rabbis.
Drew a larger crowd to hear the
dynamic exchange of ideas.
Night fell.
Jesus remained again in Jerusalem,
finding a family to let him sleep by their fire.
The next morning he went again to the temple.
Found his place among the rabbi's students.

The dialogue deep.
Rich.
Instructive.

You know the rest of the story. That day Jesus sat in the temple, astounding everyone with his understanding and his insight. Amazing the learned ones with his questions. Drawing them deeper and deeper into the scripture they often took for granted. Making them think with him. Learning more with each passing hour.

At some point, Jesus felt a heavy hand on his shoulder. Looking behind him, he saw the face of his father, a look of relieved anger etched in his eyes. Joseph said nothing. He just crooked his finger, beckoning Jesus to follow. Follow he did. They left the inner courtyard and came face to face with Mary, his mother.

The swirl of robes engulfed him amid a mother's relief of a lost child found. Then she pushed him away and the anger flashed. Jesus didn't often see his mother in such a state, but he was smart enough to know to let her speak first.

"Son, why have you treated us so? Your father and I have been looking for you anxiously."

I suspect there was more to the conversation than Luke records in his gospel. Suffice it to say, Jesus got an earful.

I also suspect there was a more sympathetic and apologetic response from Jesus than scripture records. "I am sorry. I should have asked to stay. I have never felt anything like this.

I should have asked to stay. Please don't be mad. Don't you know? *I must be about my Father's business."*

In the hugs that followed and Jesus' sincere sorrow at the distress he caused, Mary and Joseph both recall all those things they treasured in their hearts since the angel first visited. With a heavy sigh of forgiveness, Mary embraces her son again. "Please, next time, just let us know what you're doing." I can see Jesus reaching out, touching his hand to her check, a gesture of love and affection. "I'm so sorry, Mother. I promise."

As they begin again their journey home, Jesus fills each moment with excited conversation about all he had learned about God's love, God's will and God's purpose.

I think we live with the assumption that Jesus was born with the full knowledge of his God-ness. I'm not sure that's true. The day may come when I understand the duality of Jesus Christ as he lived among us as God and man. That day is not today. I reason it out as best I can, trying to rationalize the omniscient and omnipotent Father encased in human form.

We tend to see Jesus as a four-year-old boy capable of miracles, knowing completely his purpose and role as God's Messiah. Yet scripture tells us that Jesus *"grew in wisdom and stature in the eyes of men and God."* Growing in stature comes easily enough. The child became a man. Growing in wisdom complicates things. If he were God in all his complete power and knowledge from the moment of birth, why would he need to grow in wisdom?

I believe Jesus understood to whom he belonged. He knew who his Father was. His response to Mary and Joseph was honest. *"I must be about my Father's business."* I just don't think he had full knowledge of what that meant for him and how it would play out in his life. . .at least not when he was 12.

Scholars far more learned than I speak of God imposing personal limits to his own power and knowledge when he took human form so he could be "like us." Paul said as much in Philippians:

*"Though he was in the form of God, he did not count equality with God a thing to be grasped, but he **emptied himself**, taking the form of a servant."*

Perhaps Jesus emptied himself of the omniscience of the Father. There were some things he did not know. He admitted that some things were hidden from him when he told the disciples in Matthew that he did not know the day of his return:

*"Of that day and hour no one knows, not even the angels in heaven, **nor the Son**, but the Father only."*

If we can buy that idea, we see Jesus' time in the temple in a new light. Not as God speaking from the mouth of a 12-year-old, enlightening the blindness of the rabbis. Rather, we see the inquisitive nature of a student of God. One who desires to know all there is to know about the nature and work of God. One craving righteousness.

That's the point of the narrative in my eyes. Jesus preached to the multitude on the mountainside and tells them, *"Blessed are those who hunger and thirst for righteousness. . . ."* He understood the nature of that blessing because he experienced it himself as an eager boy in the temple.

He recalled that longing to know God that compelled him with passion to seek answers to questions to which he had no ready answers. The quest for righteousness drove him to study. . .to grow in spiritual wisdom. . .in preparation for the moment when God would release him for ministry.

If we are to live in the image of God, we must also hunger and thirst for righteousness as if our lives depended upon its sustenance.

What does that mean for us?

Too many Christians are not eager to understand more about God than they already know. We grow complacent and comfortable in our knowledge. As Paul said to the Corinthians, *"I gave you milk not solid food, for you were not ready for it. Indeed, you are still not ready, for you are worldly."*

It is a message echoed by the writer of Hebrews. *"Although by this time you ought to be teachers, you need someone to teach you the elementary truths of God's word all over again. . . . Everyone who lives on milk is still an infant, inexperienced in the message of righteousness."*

When we ought to be hungering for righteousness, we often grow too comfortable sitting at the kid's table, afraid of the conversations that take place in the other room. Hoping we will never be asked to sit at the big table.

Yet Jesus, as a boy, understood that obedience to God required him to open God's word. To probe and dig more deeply into its treasure. To be responsive to God's call today requires us to sink our teeth into God's scripture. Ask questions. Look for answers. Read scripture each day as if it were new. Pray that the Spirit might breathe new truth into an open heart and mind.

I am grateful for the pastors and mentors in my life. I'm grateful for parents and Sunday school teachers who challenged my thinking. Friends who encouraged me to ask questions and to keep asking until the pieces of life's puzzle began to fit together. I'm grateful to God who sometimes shows me that the puzzle pieces can fit together in a new way, taking me more deeply down the path he needs me to travel.

I am grateful that God invites us daily to sit with him at the big table.

Pull up a chair.

Let your search for righteousness begin today.

A LIFE OF INTEGRITY

Background Passage:
John 1:43-51

Gene is 92 years old, still living by himself in Levelland, Texas. He is my Dad.

Born in Rhome, Texas in 1925, my Dad grew up in a small, West Texas farming community less than 20 miles from where he lives today. He served in the Navy during World War II, spending his time in San Francisco ensuring that supplies reached their destinations on the front lines. He jokes that he served in the Navy and never set foot on a ship. After the service, he returned home, worked as a clerk in a bank until he was robbed at gunpoint and locked in the vault.

Dad spent most of his life as a cotton farmer and his later years working in the county tax appraisal district. After he retired and up until a few years ago, he delivered meals on wheels to the "old people" who couldn't make it out of the house. He still works occasionally at the appraisal district during their busy times or to help train a new worker. He spends his time trying to grow a few tomatoes in baked, red dirt that doesn't cooperate much. He does love his home-grown tomatoes, but then, so does anyone who has ever tasted home-grown tomatoes.

That tells you what he has done, but not who he is. For that, I'll simply remind you of the story of one of Jesus' disciples.

Nathaniel.
Part-time farmer.
Part-time fisherman.
Full-time seeker of God's truth.
A child of Cana,
just a few miles from Nazareth.

One day.
Nathaniel tilled the rocky soil,
preparing it for planting.
A crowded gathered on the far side of the creek
a quarter of a mile away.

Nathaniel.
Watched for a time.
Curious.
Intrigued.
Rested his chin on his hands,
gripping the top of his hoe handle.
The crowd of about 50 men, women and children
settled around a solitary man
sitting on a rock near the creek.

Nathaniel.
Wiped his brow on the sleeve of his cloak.

Took a long and satisfying drink
from his water bag.
Poured a little bit of the cool fluid on the back of his neck.
All the while staring at the peculiar assembly.

Unable to contain his rising curiosity,
Nathaniel ambled down the hill.
Jumped the small stream.
Walked to the edge of the crowd.
He marveled.
He measured
the man sitting on the rock.
Such profound words.
Different from most rabbis.
He listened as this teacher
drew the people into rich conversation
about the kingdom of God and
their place in it.

At the end of the day,
Nathaniel returned to his fields.
Continued his routine.
Shaken.
Unsettled
by all he had heard.

Several months after that first encounter,
Phillip,
a friend.
One of Jesus' new disciples.
Found Nathaniel in the market.

Face filled with urgency.
Excited beyond normal.

He pulled and dragged Nathaniel by the arm,
through the booths and the crush of people.
"Come and see," he said.
*"We have found the one whom Moses wrote about and
about whom the prophets also wrote –
Jesus of Nazareth,
the son of Joseph."*
Proclaiming the carpenter's son
as Messiah.

Well versed in scripture,
Nathaniel laughed.
He had heard this promise before.
Self-proclaimed Messiahs
who raised hopes always disappointed.

Nathaniel broke free from Phillip.
Shook his head.
Offered his verdict.
Sight unseen.
"Can anything good come out of Nazareth?"
Not a put down.
An honest question.
His "facts". . .what he knew. . .
didn't align with scripture.

Phillip persisted.
Urged him to follow.
Outside the village,

Phillip pushed past a group of men,
Nathaniel in tow.
Nathaniel stopped in his tracks.
It was the teacher he had seen months ago.

Jesus stood to greet him.
A smile and a comment
conveying immense respect.
"Here is a true Israelite in whom there is nothing false."
Such was the beginning of his friendship
with Jesus,
the teacher from Nazareth.

For the next several months,
he left his fields anytime Jesus passed through the area.
Anytime he taught in a nearby synagogue.
Listened.
Asked questions.
Shared his thoughts.
Learned.
Nathaniel found Jesus' conversations
rich with meaning and purpose.
His stories shared with the people
mesmerizing.
Penetrating.
Challenging the listener to think more
deeply about God's word.
He never left a time with this teacher
without wanting more.
Nathaniel found himself captivated by this
carpenter from Nazareth.

Whenever I think of that story and the high praise Jesus rained upon Nathaniel, I think of my Dad. The thought popped into my head again this week as we approach Father's Day. My Dad is a true child of God in whom there is nothing false. While certainly not infallible, he lives his life with the utmost integrity. What you see is what you get. And you get a whole lot of good.

As a child growing up and an adult trying to find my own way in the world, Dad's lifestyle laid out a set of undeclared expectations I still try to meet. He loved my mom completely and with full devotion. That was a gift to his three children that he modeled each day. He and my mom were affectionate, but not mushy. They endured good-natured ribbing and laughed freely. Dad was her biggest supporter, and she was his. His ability to love his wife and family openly was, and is, one of my greatest blessings in life.

Farming was not the easiest life to live. Dad would have supported any career path we chose, but we all knew his preference was for us to find another line of work. As a result, he helped raise a lawyer, a doctor and me. Dad instilled in all of his kids a serious work ethic, an attitude I see reflected in my brother and sister in the work they do. He worked hard and did what was necessary to support his family. While we may not have had a lot of material things, we were never poor. . .not in reality, nor in spirit.

Dad spent long hours in the field, but he also knew how to rest. He understood that there was a time and place for everything. He knew how to leave the worries of his work on the tractor and come home focused on his family. He could also put things beyond his control in the proper perspective. If the crop was hailed out, he spent little time moaning about his bad luck and more time thinking about the next steps. His work ethic and attitude toward life impacted me greatly.

Dad continues to teach me a great deal about our relationships to others. I don't think I have ever heard a prejudiced word escape my father's lips. Given the time period in which he grew up, that's pretty amazing. He taught all of us that a person's worth is measured by who he or she is and not where he or she comes from or what he or she looks like. Worth, to Dad, is not measured by political preferences, religious beliefs or immigrant status. A person should be measured by how life is lived each day, how others are treated, the value added to the world. To treat anyone differently is just wrong.

I watched Dad as I grew up. If he found himself in a fractured relationship for any reason, he did his best to set it right, even if it meant having difficult conversations. Most of the time, those conversations led to a deeper friendship or at least a mutual, respectful understanding of the other's position.

These things and so many others make my Dad a great man in my eyes. However, if you know my Dad or ever met him, it would not take you long to understand that his relationship to God is his greatest gift to his family and friends.

If you look back to Nathaniel's encounter with Jesus, you find Nathaniel stunned that Jesus used such kind words to describe him.

"How do you know me?"
asked Nathaniel.
Jesus replied:
"I saw you under the fig tree."

Sounds rather cryptic to us, but Bible scholars say it was not an uncommon circumstance for students of the scripture to congregate under the trees and unroll a scroll to study and discuss God's Word. I like to think that Jesus was so aware of his surroundings that Nathaniel's study under the fig tree, his desire to know God more intimately, did not go unnoticed by the Savior.

After a long day at work, it was not uncommon to see my Dad sitting in his recliner studying his Sunday school lesson while we watched Andy and Opie or some inane *Star Trek* episode. His discussions and debates with my mom about scripture were often lively and always deep.

Just reading the words of the Bible at face value is not enough for Dad. He wants to find its core meaning and its common sense application. The Bible for Dad is not spiritual pabulum or an outline of denominational theology. It is a blueprint for practical daily living. Its message drives the way he lives and loves.

I would imagine most of us raised in a Christian home could point to the lessons learned while sitting on the floor at the feet of a fantastic father. These godly men make a difference in our lives and who we grow to become. I could regale you with stories about my Dad in hopes that you would know him as I do, but I can think of nothing better than this.

Jesus recognized in Nathaniel the integrity he himself demonstrated on a daily basis. In Nathaniel, he found a man who lived a life as the image of God to the world around him. With all my heart, I believe Jesus would see the same Christ-like life lived by my Dad for almost a century.

My Dad is Nathaniel in my eyes. A man in whom there is nothing false. And I am a better man because he continues to teach me all he knows.

A LIFE OF PEACE, LOVE & JOY

Background Passages:
John 14:20-27; John 15:9-17

They sit in our utility room unopened. Last Christmas, we were asked to hold onto two gifts for my niece. One is a heart-shaped stool that belonged to her grandmother. The other is a present for my niece's daughter. My niece knows they are here. Life circumstances keep getting in the way. Like most of us, when she thinks about it, the time is not convenient to pick up the gifts. Then, it's out of sight, out of mind.

So here we are eight months later, the gifts still sit in our house, unclaimed. Hold that thought for a bit. We'll pick this up again later.

*****

What a strong sense of melancholy Jesus must have felt as he stood in the corner of the upper room listening to the light-hearted banter, a carry-over from the excitement of his triumphant entry into the city that morning. His disciples, buoyed by the throng that met them outside the gates and the welcoming shouts of praise they heard that morning, had gathered for the evening meal, exuberant and enthusiastic.

The Savior knew his inevitable fate. Knew the echoes of praise now in their ears would ring hollow in the days to come. Scripture tells us the disciples, caught up in the moment, seemed clueless as to the endgame soon to play out on a hill outside the city. Jesus stood prayerfully in that upper room. So much to say. Would they hear? Would they understand?

Over the course of the evening, the mood grew progressively more serious. More somber.

Washing of feet.
Pronouncing betrayal.
Breaking of bread.
Sharing of wine.

Gone was the fervor of the morning. In its place, confusion and concern. It was an evening filled with questions.

Peter. *"Where are you going?"*

Peter again. *"Lord, why can't I follow you now?"*

Thomas. *"Lord, we don't know where you are going, so how can we know the way?"*

Philip. *"Lord, show us the Father and that will be enough for us."*

Jesus spent these last moments available to him to teach again the truth of who he was. Offering comfort that only he could give to those who would, in a matter of hours, find their world flipped upside down. These questions are familiar to us. . .as are Jesus' answers.

To Peter. *"Where I go you cannot follow. . . ."*

To Peter again, *". . .I tell you the truth, before the rooster crows, you will disown me three times."*

To Thomas. *"I am the way, and the truth, and the life. . . ."*

To Philip: *"Anyone who has seen me has seen the Father. . .I am in the Father and the Father is in me. . ."*

In response to their growing fears, he promised that they would never be alone. That he would send a comforter and counselor. In the middle of that expansive narrative, he offered words we often forget.

"On that day, you will realize that I am in my Father, and you are in me, and I am in you."

Much of my personal Bible study over the past year has explored what it means to live in the image of God. How are we to live the Christ-like life we are called to live? Given our sinful nature, it feels almost impossible. Yet, verse after verse of scripture shows us how. . .revealed in the life of Christ. This verse offers as great a hope that I can live in God's image as any I've discovered. *". . .I am in my Father, and you are in me, and I am in you."*

Living in the image of God is as simple as allowing Jesus, who is in us, to be the boss of our lives. To take control of every aspect of them. Of course, that's easier said than done. I know. I fail miserably at it each day, it seems. Yet the greater possibility exists that I can respond to the challenges of this world as God would like for me to respond because his presence in my life is a constant.

Give that some thought. He is *in* me. He is *in* you.

As the narrative in John 14 and 15 continued, Jesus touched upon three attributes of his life that he gifts to us when we place our trust in him. These teachings stem from yet another question asked by a disciple we don't hear from often. . .Judas, not Iscariot, sometimes called Thaddaeus.

"Lord, why do you intend to show yourself to us, but not to the world?"

Thaddaeus had missed the point. Jesus tried explaining to him and the other disciples that he reveals himself completely to those who call upon him. Those who place their faith in him. Those who love him. People who live by the world will never understand Jesus until they open their hearts to him.

The teachable moment continued. Jesus gave us more insight into his character, offering that which he possessed to his disciples, and by extension, to us. It comes as a gift, one we will need to accept if we are to live like Christ.

"Peace I leave with you. My peace I give to you. I do not give to you as the world gives. Do not let your hearts be troubled and do not be afraid."

The world's idea of peace is the absence of conflict. We know from Jesus' life that living as he lived will not end struggle, but may in fact, add to it. Jesus said *"My peace I give you."* What is the peace he gives? William Barclay says it conveys the idea that we have all we need for our "highest good." He wrote, "The peace the world offers is the peace of escape, peace that comes from the avoidance of trouble." The peace Jesus offers, Barclay says, is the peace which "no experience of life can take from us." A peace that is not dependent on life's circumstances.

Jesus lived his whole life under the shelter of this peace woven into his spiritual DNA. It was an essential part of who he was. Despite all he was sent to do and all he had to endure, Jesus' spirit was never threatened.

His peace is part and parcel of the gift of salvation. As he lives in us, his peace is gifted to us. Not just any peace, but *his* peace. The same spirit of peace that carried him through every temptation, every trial, every test exists within us as his gift to those who know him. We just have to claim it and remove it from its box, allowing it to pervade every corner of our being. Living in the image of God, in the image of Christ, means abiding in his peace.

A few verses later in Chapter 15, Jesus continued his teaching to the troubled disciples. He asked them to picture a grapevine, declaring himself the vine and urging them to see themselves as the branches that can and must bear fruit.

Buried in that familiar passage is another verse that speaks to the very nature of Jesus Christ. Jesus personified love. It motivated everything he said and everything he did. He felt the all-encompassing love of his father and passed that love on to those he encountered. Love filled his heart and soul.

"As the father has loved me, so I have loved you. Now remain in my love. . .love each other as I have loved you."

He revealed the depth of his love for those who believe in him. . ."*as the father has loved me so I have loved you.*" He loved his disciples, he loves us, with all the love the Creator holds for his created. It is not that way in a world without Christ. The world loves until it is disappointed. The world's love turns quickly to ambivalence or hate again, based on outside circumstances.

Jesus told his disciples to remain in his love. What is Jesus' love? He provided an illustration.

"Greater love has no man than this, but to lay down his life for a friend."

We are called to love one another. That's not just a call to love other Christians. We are called to extend God's love to our fellow man. Few of us may be called to mortally sacrifice our lives for another as Jesus did. Each of us, however, is called to personally sacrifice in service to those in need. Such selfless sacrifice provides evidence of our love.

The great news is that because he abides in us, we don't need to rely on our human capacity to love. We get to draw from the deep well of God's all-encompassing love within us. What a gift!

We see in the scripture that God has given us his peace and his love. He didn't stop there. He urged his disciples to remain obedient to all he had taught them; to all God called them to do. Obedience to God's will opens his gift of joy.

"I have told you this so my joy may be in you and that your joy may be complete."

Living as the world lives is easy. It requires little stamina. One just floats with the flow. Jesus told his disciples that his way was hard. Living in the image of God, standing firm in faith, demands we swim against the prevailing current. Yet, despite the difficulty surrounding the Christian journey, the path we follow ought to be joyous.

There is always joy in doing the right thing. Joy in living a purposeful life. Joy in letting Christ control your day-to-day living. In knowing you have been true to the commands of Christ.

Jesus lived his life on earth as the personification of peace, love and joy. These fruits of the spirit were embedded within his nature. They are part of the image we hold of him. A part of who he was as a man. Despite the rigors of his mission and ministry, no outward circumstance would ever strip from him that essential part of his spirit and personality.

Peace.

Love.

Joy.

Those life-sustaining characteristics he embraced are now embedded in all who believe in his name. He promised it! *"You are in me and I am in you."* He gifted his peace, his love and his joy to each of us.

Here's the thing. It's not just that he put the capacity to experience these things into our hearts for us to develop and grow. His peace, love and joy reside within us already fully developed and available through the presence of the Holy Spirit. The indwelling presence of Christ in the form of the Holy Spirit gives us access to the heart of Jesus. To the all-to-often untapped potential and power of Christ in us.

To his peace.
To his love.
To his joy.

These great gifts sit in the utility room of our hearts waiting to be claimed. They will never be enjoyed and experienced until we pick them up. Take them home. Put them to good use. Our unclaimed gifts of God's Spirit keep us from living as the image of God.

Jesus said, *"My peace, my love and my joy I give to you."*

Maybe, just maybe, it's time we opened the package.

A LIFE OF COMPASSION

Background Passages:
Luke 10:25-37; Mark 12:28-34; Matthew 7:12

"What must I do to inherit eternal life?"
A seminal question.
Shouted by an expert in the law.
Challenging.
Confrontational.
Combative.

Jesus.
Engaged in intimate conversation with a small crowd
that gathered around the Galilean teacher.
All conversation stopped.
Heads turned toward the booming voice
from the edge of the crowd.
The Pharisee hiked up his flowing robe.
Pushed himself away from the large rock he leaned against.
Moved forward until he towered over Jesus
sitting on a fallen cedar log.

The man's presence had not gone unnoticed by Jesus.

He had skirted the periphery of the crowd for the past
three days.
Listening without hearing.
Rolling his eyes.
Biting his tongue.
Biding his time.
Just one among a small group of Pharisees
tracking Jesus from
Jericho to Jerusalem.

They weren't following the teacher through the
harsh environment of the desert to understand
Jesus and his teaching.
They followed to find fault in his words.

to discredit him in the eyes of the people.
The scribe asked the most important question,
but it lacked in sincerity.
Uttered by one loving the sound of his own voice.
Seeking a specific answer.
Hoping for something heretical.

Jesus.
Looked at the man for a moment.
Sensing without question the twisted intent of his heart.
Still,
he smiled.
"What does the law say?
How do you read it?"

Giving the man his moment in the spotlight.
Guiding the man's inevitable conclusion.

The scribe turned confidently to the crowd.
Proclaimed with complete assurance
"'Love the Lord your God with all your heart and
with all your soul and
with all your strength and
with all your mind; and
'love your neighbor as yourself.'"
Smug.
Self-satisfied.
He turned back to face Jesus,
daring him to disagree.

"You're absolutely right."
"Do this and you will have eternal life."
Jesus sat silently. Eyes never wavering from the
eyes of the Pharisee.
The silence between them deepened.
The scribe shuffled his feet.
Not getting the answer he expected from the teacher.
His eyes flashed as he fell back on his legal training.
Focusing his attack from a different angle.
"Ahh, and just who is my neighbor?"

Jesus pursed his lips.
Let out a slow breath through his nostrils.
For all he understood of God's greatest commandments,
the man limited God's universal truth
by qualifying its spirit.
"Let me tell you a story. . ."

*****

W hat Jesus speaks next is perhaps one of the most well-known parables he ever shared. The parable of the Good Samaritan transcends religious conversation, working its way into secular contexts. Good Samaritan laws protect those who lend assistance in life-threatening situations. Those who go out of their way to help another are called good Samaritans.

Here's the gist of the story Jesus told.

A man traveling alone from Jerusalem to Jericho was attacked by robbers who beat him senseless and took his clothes and his money. They threw him into the ditch next to the road, bleeding, broken and near death. At separate times, a Jewish priest and a temple administrator happened upon the scene of the crime. They pretended not to see the man lying in the ditch. They averted their eyes. Shuffled to the other side of the road. Quickened their pace. Disregarded the man in distress. Out of sight, out of mind.

Later, a Samaritan on his way to Jericho came across the bleeding man. Compassion ruled the moment, and the Samaritan jumped into the ditch to render aid. He cleaned the man's cuts and bruises with his oil and wine. Tore the hem of his garment to bandage the man's wounds. He lifted the injured man onto his own donkey and walked him miles into the city. He took the man to an inn. Nursed his needs throughout the night. The next morning, the Samaritan paid the innkeeper to watch over the man, promising to cover any additional costs the innkeeper incurred when the Samaritan returned.

Jesus told the story to the crowd gathered around him. He looked into the faces of every person listening. Finally, his eyes bore into the eyes of the scribe still standing in the middle. Jesus' eyes narrowed. His voice lowered an octave. His next question landed like a heavy weight upon the man's chest, crushing the breath from his lungs.

"Which of these three do you think was a neighbor to the man who fell into the hands of the robbers?"

I picture the man stuttering and stammering before falling silent, fully aware that he had been outfoxed by the master teacher. His brain flashed in overdrive as he tried to think of a snappy comeback. Unable to give credit to a hated Samaritan, he answered in little more than a grudging whisper.

"The one who showed mercy on him."

The lengthy conversation between Jesus and the Pharisee must have inspired those who sat around as they watched it unfold. The parable shared by Jesus subtly suggested that faith is best demonstrated not by grand theological arguments, but by the things we do for others. And it is a message that echoes loudly today. A lesson I still need to learn at times.

Here's the thing. The scribe asked a great question in the beginning. It is the fundamental question all of us who long for meaning in life should ask. *"How do I find eternal life?"*

Ironically, the Pharisee gave the same answer that Jesus gave to another group of Pharisees who questioned him about God's greatest commandments (Mark 12:28-34). Had the man stopped to consider the meaning and spirit of the words he uttered, the whole conversation might have taken a different and better turn.

His second question, however, revealed an exclusionary faith. *"Who is my neighbor?"* is a question that sought only to limit our compassion. . .creating boundaries that give us an out. *"Who is my neighbor?"* suggests that some groups or some individuals are unworthy of my time and effort.

The religious leader practiced a ritualized religion based on man-made rules that identified peoples that the law considered unclean and unworthy of God's love. The Pharisees and scribes knew Jesus frequently associated with tax collectors, Samaritans, Gentiles, lepers, outcasts and outlaws. When the scribe asked his question, I suspect he hoped Jesus might identify as a neighbor one among this group of the unclean that Jewish law excluded from fellowship.

We often fall into the same trap as the scribe. Surely my "neighbor" only includes those people with whom I have a relationship. . .those who look like me. . .those who live in my social circle. . .my own racial subset. . .those to whom I can give money, but not get my hands dirty. . .those whose needs do not inconvenience me.

Jesus rejected that view. In Jesus' parable, the Samaritan showed compassion and mercy to the injured man even though society considered the Samaritan an outcast and unworthy of God's love. So, from Jesus' standpoint, the question is not *"Who is my neighbor,"* but rather, "Whose neighbor can I be?"

It's not a matter of identifying the person I wish to help. It's a matter of looking for the unfolding opportunities God places before me to serve my God and my fellow man. Determining whose neighbor I can be demands that I step outside my comfort zone. . .insists that I engage with those whose backgrounds and cultures differ significantly from mine. . .mandates that I move past the safety of simple charitable giving to immerse myself in the gritty world of need in which others live.

Jesus defined our "neighbor" when he addressed the Pharisees in Mark. *"Love your neighbor as you love yourself."* Find the definition also encompassed in the Golden Rule. *"Do unto others (your neighbor) as you would have others do unto you."*

Both verses suggest an empathy that allows us to see ourselves in the circumstances experienced by someone else. Except for the grace of God, we could find ourselves in similar circumstances. That realization should compel us to provide the same help and assistance to another in need that we desire in our most desperate times.

In essence, Jesus asked the Pharisee to abandon the smooth road of ritualized religion and live in the dirty ditch of practical and powerful faith. Forget about qualifying those we choose to help. Look instead for the chance to change the course of another's life.

It's a good question.

Whose neighbor can you be?

A LIFE OF DEEPLY ROOTED FAITH

Background Passages:
Matthew 13:1-23; Mark 4:1-20; Luke 8:1-15

"Like locusts,"
Peter marveled,
"descending on a field of grain."
The disciple commented on the crowd
gathering for the Master's teaching.
Another day.
Another multitude.

James.
A disciple of Christ.
The son of Alphaeus.
Not the fisherman.
Raised his head.
Glanced back at the mass of humanity
spreading out across the mountain.
Muttered his agreement.
"Give them credit.
They've come a long way in this heat

just to hear his words of wisdom."

James watched Jesus working his way
among the crowd.
So full of energy.
Eager to engage each person on a personal level.

Stretching as far as he could see,
hundreds of men, women and children
congregated on the dusty hillside.

Turned its landscape into a
blossoming field of flowing robes.
Stretching their necks to catch a glimpse of the man who. . .
worked miracles.
Fed thousands.
Healed the infirmed.
Spoke more clearly than any rabbi.
James shook his head in wonder.
Leaned heavily against the prow of the boat.
He and Peter
pushed the small fishing vessel
into the warm waters of the Sea of Galilee.
Gave their Master a platform from which to speak.

The multitude settled at last to
understand more about
the carpenter turned rabbi.
Many shouted out.
Sought answers to their most pressing questions.
"Who are you exactly?"
"Why are you here?"

"What must we do?"
Questions James had heard since the
Jewish leaders began their disinformation campaign
accusing Jesus of every type of
heresy under the law.

James watched.
Jesus waited
for the tide of questions to ebb.

Amid the silence of anticipation,
Jesus pointed to the distant hillside.
"See that farmer?"
The crowd turned to look.
James chuckled under his breath,
at the sound of rustling robes turning in unison.

The Farmer.
Stood hunched over against the weight of the
heavy seed bag tied around his waist.
Every two or three steps, he stopped.
Dipped his hand into the bag.
With a casual and practiced flick of his wrist,
he cast seeds across his small plot of land.

"My work is much like his,"
said Jesus.
"Sowing seeds of God's truth to those who will hear."
As the crowd turned back, he asked,
"Will you listen?"
"A farmer went out to sow his seed. . ."
James sat at Jesus' feet as he always did.

Mesmerized
by every word.
Marveled
that the simplest illustration could hold such
elaborate truth.
Awestruck
that Jesus could pull a lesson of
eternal value from the
most mundane acts of life.

*****

Sermon ended.
Service began.
Jesus and the disciples moved through the crowd.
Helping in any and every way they could.

James thought about the parable
throughout the day as he worked.
Unsettled.
Uncertain.
Uneasy.
He had missed something.
Was sure of it.

At last,
the crowd dispersed.
Jesus sat around the campfire surrounded by
his most trusted followers.
Exhausted from the day's ministry.
As was their habit,
they sat around the campfire. . .

Talking quietly.

Reflecting privately.

Discussing intimately.

Debating the meaning and intent of the words they heard.

Jesus.

Sat against a fig tree.

Arms across his chest.

Head back.

Eyes closed.

Listening,

but not looking.

James.

Shuffled from group to group.

Listened without comment

to the conversations.

Processed inwardly what he heard.

He found himself standing beside the tree where Jesus sat.

More nervous than usual when alone with Jesus.

Kicked the toe of his sandal against a root.

Hoped Jesus would notice his presence.

Finally, he cleared his voice.

"Jesus.

Are you asleep?"

Jesus.

Didn't move a muscle.

A rueful grin broke across his face.

One weary eye opened.

One eyebrow raised.

"I wish!" He groaned.

Glancing up at the young disciple,
"What do you need,
my friend?"
James looked sheepishly at the others around the fire,
feeling inside that they knew things he did not know.
"That parable you told today. . .
about the farmer. . .
what exactly did it mean?"
Jesus arched his back.
Pushed away from the trunk of the tree.
Grasped his knees and pulled them to his chest.
Speaking in a voice loud enough for all the disciples to hear,
"Among all men, you are fortunate.
The secrets of the Kingdom of God have been revealed to you."
James chuckled.
The rustle of their robes
reminded him of the crowd on the hillside.
Closing his eyes as if thinking of the multitude,
Jesus shook his head.
"The others. . .
the people. . .
I speak in parables to help them understand.
So they can see what they may not see.
Hear what they may not understand."

He paused for a moment.
Searched their eyes.
Sensed their uncertainty.
"This is what the parable means. . ."
The explanation.

Lengthy, but to the point.

The disciples listened.
Some nodded in agreement.
Some probed with further questions.
James sat silently.
Getting the point,
but still sensing a gap in his understanding.
Innate shyness prevented him from pushing for clarity.

Later.
Jesus leaned again,
alone against his tree.
The others congregated in small clusters around the camp.
Again in quiet conversation.

James.
Paced the edge of darkness.
Hands behind his back.
Deep in thought.
He found himself once again
standing beside the tree.
Silent.
Still.

Jesus again wearily opened one eye.
Raised one eyebrow.
Smiled slightly at the timid intrusion.
Spoke in a quiet, reassuring voice.
"Something bothering you, James?"

The young disciple

leaned against the tree.
Facing east to Jesus' south.
Slid quietly to the ground.

Let the course bark scratch his back.
He settled in silence into a comfortable spot.
Always patient,
Jesus waited for his friend to speak.

After a moment, James said,
"I get most of it, I think.
You're the farmer. . .at work in your world.
The seed. . .God's truth.
His word.
The different kinds of soil. . .
hearers of his word.
Hard.
Rocky.
Thorny.
Fertile."

James paused again,
unsure of his next thought.
James pressed Jesus for clearer understanding.
Deeper insight.
About the soil. . .
the listeners.
"How can they hear the same word so differently?"

"What do you think?" Jesus asked.

"The hard soil.
On the surface,
no pun intended," he smiled.
"It seems to talk about the. . .
determined opponent of God.
Disinterested in godly things.
Hard. Bitter.
Beaten down by life.
Refusing to let any ounce of truth penetrate the surface.
Hardened to any possibility of faith.
An unbeliever.

"But I think there's more to it than that."
Turning to Jesus, he said,
"Isn't it possible a person could be so wrapped up in
doing good
that he may no longer hear a new word from God?
So focused on his ministry that he
misses other opportunities to serve?"

Jesus.
Eyes still closed.
He said,
"True enough.
Look at the Pharisees.

So busy with ritual they never get to know God intimately.
So involved in 'worship' they never
practice what they preach.
"Worship must be personal.
Must breech the hardness of our hearts,

or it's meaningless."

Encouraged,
James pressed on.
"The soil on top of rocky ground. . .
enough sustenance to sprout.
Not enough to grow.
Some listeners,
excited about the work of God,
try to live it daily.
Yet when crisis comes,
when they fall upon hard times,
they fall away.
Faith withers and dies."

Jesus nodded.
"We must be grounded,
rooted in our faith,
to withstand the difficulties
we inevitably face.
Life is not easy."
Jesus continued.
"A true life of faith is even more difficult.
Setting our roots means we must be so grounded
in our study of God's word that we never lack for
spiritual nourishment that sustains."

James quietly quoted something Jesus said
in another time.
Another place.
"If I say I love God and don't evidence it in my life,

I'm a liar."

Jesus laughed.
"You have been listening!"

The two men sat in silence for a while as James thought
deeply about what Jesus said.
The disciple took another deep breath.
"Let's talk about the third soil. . .

Full of weeds and thorns.
Choking the life out of the good grain.
Bad attitudes and actions strangle life.
Good intentions get choked out by disbelief."
James.
Energized.
Engaged.
Eager.
Sat cross legged facing Jesus.
Hands gesturing to punctuate his excitement.

"Lives get smothered by things that ultimately don't matter.
We nit-pick each other over inconsequential things.
Kill our own spirit and the
spirits of those around us."

Jesus.
Fully awake and animated
mirrored James' posture.
Cross legged and leaning toward his friend.

He reached across the distance between them.
Slapped him on the knees.

"Now, you're getting it!"

Jesus added,
"There is a tendency to lose the joy of salvation.
The dogs of life nip at our heels.
We let bias and prejudice get in the way of loving
relationships.
Arguments over things. . .
great or small. . .
just don't matter in the end.
They choke our relationships.
Get in the way of our ability to love one another.
Jesus's eyes danced.

"Go on, James," he urged,
"What about the good soil?"
James sat for a minute.
Stunned that he was enmeshed in this conversation.
"The good soil. . .

Fertile.
Rich.
Bountiful.
Represents those of us who get it.
Those who understand what God desires of us.
Those who understand more clearly who *you* are.
Those who take part in the harvest.
Bringing people to know *you*.
To accept *your* truth."

Jesus.
Shook his head.

"Think, James.
It's deeper than that.
Keep digging."

James found himself. . .
Prodded.
Probed.
Propelled beyond
convenience and conventional wisdom.
His mind raced.
Vaguely aware that others had gathered around.
Listening intently to the dialogue.

His finger punched in frustration at the ground beneath him.
"I don't understand.
You're not making sen. . . ."

James stopped in mid-sentence.
Sat back.
Mouth hanging open.
His mind processing a new thought.
Quietly.
Thinking aloud.

"The farmer broadcast his seed in the field.
The field. . .
the field. . . .
It's the same field. . . .

All of the soils.
Hard packed.
Shallow.

Thorny.
Fertile.
They're all in the same field!"
Jesus leaned in. . .
Broad smile on his face. . .
"Sooooo. . .?"

James looked at Jesus.
Tears of understanding welled in his eyes.
"They're all me.
Every soil is me.
It's not about how the multitude responds to the gospel,
it's about how I respond.

"I can be at times too hard. . .
too busy even *in* service to be *of* service.
I can be shallow and artificial in faith. . .
fainting at the first sign of adversity.
I can be overly concerned with things
that don't matter in God's grand scheme.
Hypercritical of others.
Or. . .
I can be productive,
fertile. . .
fully responsive
to the will of God in my life."

Jesus looked at James.
Eyes sympathetic and understanding.
"Knowing our capacity for failure is the
first step in avoiding the pitfalls.

Like I said before,
*'All have sinned and fallen short of the
glory of God.'"*

James wiped away tears with the sleeve of his tunic.
Embarrassed by his display of emotion.

Jesus.
Grasped the hand of his disciple.
Firm and reassuring.
"Don't worry about the tears, James.
You're in the good soil now.
You're just watering your roots."

*****

I'm not sure about you. This parable speaks to my faith. . . crisply and clearly. Identifying my life, at best, as a spasmodic attempt to respond to the call of God.

Any honest evaluation of my life shows that I am sometimes self-absorbed. Too busy *acting* good, rather than *doing* good. At other times, I am false and artificial, exhibiting a *show* of faith without the *substance* of faith.

Then, at still other times, I grow hypocritical, judging the speck of sawdust in the eyes of others while ignoring the 2x4 plank in my own.

Thank God there are times when I am fertile and productive in my actions for Christ, sinking my roots into the deep, loamy soil of God's truth. Fully responsive to his will.

I just don't think Jesus ever stopped listening to the voice of his Father, God. Around every corner, the Pharisees laid a trap to catch him off his game. To draw him into a debate in which he would say something that would indict him as a troublemaker and heretic.

Every obstacle he faced was an opportunity to sin. . .to go his own way and abandon the will of his Father. God's spirit within, his time in prayerful conversation with the Father, kept him focused. Kept his roots firmly planted in the soil of God's purpose and plan.

If we are to mirror Christ in all we do, we too must ground ourselves firmly in God's purpose and plan for our lives.

My prayer, for me and for you, is that we find time to listen to the voice of God's Spirit that tells us we are missing something important in God's word. To find the courage to sit at the tree where Jesus sits, asking for clarity and understanding. To dig deeper into familiar scripture. To grow our roots deeply into the fertile soil of his truth.

May our tears of understanding water the roots of our faith.

A LIFE OF EMPATHY

Background Passages:
Hebrews 13:3; Luke 6:31-36; Philippians 2:5-8

C ecil Rhodes, the British statesman and financier who used his wealth to endow the famous Rhodes Scholarship, had a reputation for his elegant fashion sense and impeccable dress. One year, Rhodes invited one of his scholarship recipients to his home to dine with him and a number of England's well-to-do.

The young man came from a poor family. He wore his best suit to dinner, though stained and a little too small. He was embarrassed upon his arrival to find all the other guests in full evening dress. Rhodes, dressed in his tuxedo, was about to enter the dining room when he saw the young man and his discomfort. He went back upstairs, appearing at the dining table a few minutes later in a shabby, old blue suit.

Rhodes understood the distress the young man felt. Rather than add to the misery of another, he set aside his personal preference to connect with this young man of promise.

Empathy.

Empathy feels what another feels. Sees the world from another's perspective. Understands as fully as possible what another experiences. It is one thing to feel, see and understand the life of another. It's a great first step. But, it seems to me, true empathy compels us to act. . .to walk an extra mile.

We can imagine the horror experienced by the family whose home is wiped out by flood or fire. We have difficulty at times imaging the struggles of the learning disabled when learning comes easily to us. We struggle in our response to those who are depressed if we ourselves have never experienced hopelessness. Empathy is difficult.

Empathy is also inconvenient, especially when life is going our way. I can see the plight of the poor and the afflicted but do not wish to sully my hands with the work it would take to help them work through their own difficulties. We rationalize the distance we keep by blaming them for their own predicament.

As he closed out his letter, the writer of Hebrews exhorted believers to "Remember those in prison as if you were their fellow prisoners and those who are mistreated as if you yourselves were suffering."

Those encouragements go far beyond simply feeling sorrow or sympathy *for* those who are troubled. It calls upon us to feel *with* them as if the suffering were our own. To put ourselves in their shoes. To see the world. . .and ourselves. . .through their eyes.

Jesus, the personification of God's empathy toward a lost world, shows us the full expression of empathy as he introduces to us his concept we know as the Golden Rule.

"Do unto others as you would have them do unto you."

He taught that one could sum up the entire content of the Old Testament law and prophets by doing to others what you would have them do to you. To act in ways toward others as you wish others to act toward you.

The concept Jesus introduced was not a new concept. Many other religions and philosophies offer a similar message, though often presented in negative form. In ancient Egypt, the statement read, "That which you hate to be done to you, do not do to another." In ancient Greece, "Do not do to others that which angers you when they do it to you." Self-preservation is not empathy.

When Jesus asks us to treat others as we want to be treated, he is not saying: I'll scratch your back if you'll scratch mine. It's so much more than that. It is a proactive directive.

Empathy takes pre-emptive action to meet the needs of others because we feel the distress as if it were our own. So we act, treating others as we would hope others would treat us if we found ourselves in similar circumstances.

We're not simply to avoid doing things that hurt others because we don't want to be hurt in the same way. Instead, every action toward others should be expressed in the love of Christ. He's saying: Take the risk of giving your time, your energy, your resources. . .in essence, giving yourself. .

.to ease the pain of another, whether that person is a friend or stranger.

Jesus followed this command by telling us how to live an empathetic life. He explained,

"If you love those who love you, what credit is that to you? And if you do good to those who are good to you, what credit is that to you? Even 'sinners' do that. . .Love your enemies, do good to them, and lend to them without expecting to get anything in return. Be merciful (other translations use the words "compassionate," "empathetic"), *just as your Father is merciful."*

Living a Christ-like life teaches us that religion and faith are not just a set of beliefs. They are not the dogma of the day. Christianity, if it is to be viable and real in our lives, is about what we do for the poor with too little to eat, too little to wear and little or no shelter over their heads. It is about what we do for the sick and the elderly, in desperate need of our touch. It is about what we do for the disenfranchised of society who find themselves distanced from the opportunities we enjoy.

Jesus teaches us that empathy, as difficult and inconvenient as it can be at times, ought to compel us to act differently when we encounter human need. To understand the needs of others as if they were our own.

We have the perfect example in the life of Christ. Paul said as much to the Philippian church.

"Your attitude should be the same as Christ Jesus: Who, being in very nature God, did not consider equality with God something to

be grasped, but made himself nothing, taking the very nature of a servant being made in human likeness."

Leaving the throne of God to become God in human form is the ultimate act of empathy. A deliberate, purposeful, life-giving act of empathy that led straight to the cross.

Today, it seems most people walk the world blind to the feelings and needs of others. If they disagree with us, if they live differently from us, if they respond to the challenges they face in ways we would not, we chastise them for not reacting as we assume we would react in similar circumstances. I'm not sure we will ever impact the world for Christ until we can walk a mile in their shoes.

I hope God challenges all of us this week to embrace the empathy of Christ as we encounter the needs of the world around.

LIKE FATHER, LIKE SON

Background Passages:
John 14:5-14; I John 2:5-6; Matthew 11:28-30

"So God created mankind in his own image, in the image of God he created them; male and female he created them." (Genesis 1:27)

Michelangelo did his best to capture the image of God on the plaster of the Sistine Chapel in Rome. . .a gray-headed man with a flowing gray beard, reaching out to touch the extended hand of man as he reaches for the Father-God. Maybe that's the mental image we all have of God. Zeus on a grander scale. Maybe we're missing the point.

Being created in the image of God seems a hard concept for us to grasp. We know it's not a physical thing, but to be created in the spiritual mold of God eludes us as well. Trapped in the twisted realities of our own making, it's hard to see how we can be like God. It wasn't any easier for Jesus' disciples, and they, and the thousands of souls Jesus encountered during his time on earth, had the best chance to make the connection because he was standing right in front of them.

Join me as a fly on the wall of the upper room. . .

*****

Day's darkness descends,
checked by the soft light of oil lamps
sending tendrils of black smoke curling toward the ceiling.
The smell of smoke mingled with the
fragrant oil used to wash the feet of the disciples.

Peter.
Hunched over.
Head down.
Hands trembling with
embarrassment and dread.
Mind disjointed. . .
a jumble of discordant thoughts.
The evening stood in stark contrast
to the glory experienced that afternoon.

His Teacher.
Riding the winding road down the Kidron Valley
past the ancient cemetery.
Through the olive groves.
Pushing through the gathered crowds
shouting "Hosannas."
Singing praises.
Calling for God's blessing upon
"the king of Israel."

His Teacher.
Now,
in the upper room,
a sobering and surreal silence

replaced the post-Jerusalem-entry giddiness
as each disciple
felt the calloused hands of their master
as he washed their feet in
warm water and
fragrant oil.

What followed
darkened the mood deeper than the descending night.
Judas' whispered and abrupt dismissal.
Jesus' implied admission of his impending death.
Peter's confusion.
Jesus' accusation of a night of betrayal.

Jesus' words of comfort
did little to offset Peter's angst.
The warmth of the fire
did little to take away the chill that brought shivers.
He pulled his cloak more tightly around himself.

Jesus.
"Do not let your hearts be troubled.
Trust in God, trust also in me.
. . .I am going to prepare a place for you. . . .
I will come back and take you to be with me. . . .
. . .You know the way. . ."

Peter.
Thoughts interrupted by the confused questions of
his friends.
Questions that echoed in his own mind.

First, Thomas.
"Lord, we don't know where you are going,
so how can we know the way?"

Jesus.
"I am the way,
the truth,
the life.
No one comes to the Father except through me.
If you really knew me,
you would know the Father."

Then, Philip.
"Lord, show us the Father.
That will be enough for us."

Jesus.
"Anyone who has seen me has seen the Father.
Don't you believe that I am in the Father and the
Father is in me?"

*****

And there it is. The crux. The nitty gritty. The bottom line. The heart of the gospel's good news. *"Anyone who has seen me has seen the Father."* Or, as Jesus says to a group of challenging Pharisees in John 10, *"I and the Father are One."*

Follow my circuitous logic. Genesis tells us we are *"created in the image of God."* Do not get caught up in a physical appearance. The Bible speaks of a spiritual connection. We are God's children. His family. He designed us with the spiritual DNA that would enable us to live in relationship with the one willing to walk with us in the first garden.

His likeness.
His image.

He created us as beings capable of God's compassion.

God's forgiveness.
God's justice.
God's love.

Our sin broke the connection. Smudged the image God desired to see reflected in the mirrored likeness he created. Our failures diminished our capacity to relate to his created world as his hands, his voice and his heart.

So God worked through time, preparing his choice creation for a moment in Bethlehem when he would insert himself into our history. To be with us. God in the world. At that point in time, God sent a baby that would grow into a man and live as an example of the very character and nature of God.

Jesus, wrapped in flesh. Fragile and frail. As he grew, he would be tempted to take his own path in every way as we are tempted to run from the Father who created us. In other words, Jesus would become so very. . .human. Yet, at the same time, through a life of obedience to the will of God, Jesus fault-lessly revealed the character of God. A picture-perfect human representation of the image of God.

Can you imagine the disappointment Jesus must have felt in his last hours when he tried to prepare them for what was to come? Three years he had taught them and still they didn't get it. *"If you really knew me, Phillip, you would know the Father."*

But, then, how am I any different? "If you really knew me, Kirk, you would know the Father."

Ok. I get it. God is Christ. Christ is God. To know Jesus is to know God.

What's the point of the exercise? Putting faith and trust in Jesus Christ as God's Son opens the path of salvation. I am saved at a point in time. I am living out that salvation today, knowing that my eternal salvation waits for my death. I delight in that concept. Saved and always saved.

Sadly, that first step is the only step some people take. God does not just call us to salvation. His call demands that we live that salvation daily. . .that we become more like Christ. . . .

In the way we act.
In the way we think.
In the way we treat others.
In the way we remain obedient to God's will.

The Apostle Paul says it this way to the Ephesians: *"Be imitators of God, therefore, as dearly loved children and live a life of love. . . ."* He echoes the same sentiment to the Corinthians: *"Follow my example as I follow the example of Christ."*

The implication for my life. . .for your life. . .is real and profound. As a child of God, I am to be like Christ.

Morally.
Mentally.
Socially.
Spiritually.

In my daily life, I must model Jesus by filling my heart and mind with his teachings and his thoughts. In my relationship with the world around me, I must model Jesus.

Live my life as he lived.
Touch my fellow man as he touched.
Serve others as he served.

John encouraged his readers to follow in the footsteps of Christ. He wrote,

"If anyone obeys his word, God's love is truly made complete in him. This is how we know we are in him. Whoever claims to live in him must walk as Jesus walked."

God created me to be the mirror image of Christ in a lost and hurting world, recognizable through my life work. Christ in me.

We best understand who he was. . .who he is. . .who he wants us to be. . . by learning how he lived. And that's the challenge before us. To walk each day as he walked in absolute faith and devotion to the Father.

That path and its demands seem. . .

Demoralizing.

Daunting.

Difficult.

Jesus suggests otherwise.

"Come to me, all you who are weary and burdened, and I will give you rest. Take my yoke upon you and learn from me, for I am gentle and humble in heart, and you will find rest for your souls. For my yoke is easy and my burden is light."

We must learn from the master teacher by emulating those character traits he demonstrated daily. Live as he lived. Walk as he walked. We must trust in faith that the burden is light; the task not too difficult.

So let's look at the stories in scripture. I mean, really look at the stories. Discover the one who created us in his own image. Discover the one who is God. Live as he lived so the world sees Jesus in us.

I am created in the image of God. . .

to live.

to love.

I am created in the image of God. . .

to be his voice,

his hands.

his heart.

I am created in the image of God. . .

to be Jesus

in a lost and hurting world.

ABOUT THE AUTHOR

K nown as a storyteller throughout his career in public education and as a teacher in Sunday school, Dr. Kirk Lewis has authored two books of devotional stories, *Put Away Childish Things* in 2013 and *The Chase: Our Passionate Pursuit of Life Worth Living* in 2014. Drawing positive reviews for their messages and imaginative writing style, both books are almost guaranteed to make you look at your favorite Bible stories in a new light. *Put Away Childish Things* won a Christian Writers Award in 2014.

Lewis has taught Sunday school to adults for more than 40 years and serves as an ordained deacon at South Main Baptist Church in Pasadena, Texas. As a student at Texas Tech University, he served as a youth minister at First Baptist Church, Wolfforth, Texas before attending Southwestern Baptist Theological Seminary in Fort Worth to pursue a degree in religious education.

Lewis and his wife Robin have two sons, two daughters-in-law and four delightful grandchildren. All are active members of South Main Baptist Church.

Lewis continues to provide regular and creative Bible studies on his blog *The Searcher*. You can find out more about the author and his other books by visiting his website at www.drkirklewis.com.

CPSIA information can be obtained
at www.ICGtesting.com
Printed in the USA
LVHW021922261118
598271LV00009B/596